Python Programming

A Complete Python Guide To Introduction You In Programming With Exercise, Projects and Solution

By

Aiden Phillips

Table of Contents

Introduction:

Python is a high-level programming language that is dynamically interpreted, symantic and object-oriented. Its high-level already present data structures, together with dynamic typing and dynamic binding, making it ideal for Software Development and as a glue language or scripting for the purpose of linking current components. Python's concise, easy-to-learn syntax prioritizes readability, which maintenance expenses for software. Packages and modules are supported by Python, which fosters code reuse and program modularity. An interpreter of python including its substantial standard libraries are available for free to download and disperse in binary or source type for all main sites.

Python has become a first-class citizen in contemporary infrastructure management, software development, and data analysis during the last several years. This is no more aside utility language, but instead a significant force in online application development and systems administration, as well as a primary driver of the machine intelligence and big data analytics explosions.

Python is popular among programmers because of the enhanced productivity it offers. The edit test debug cycle is extraordinarily rapid because there is no compiling phase. Python scripts are simple to debug: a bug or improper input will never result in a segmentation fault. However, when an interpreter finds a mistake, it throws an exception. The interpreter produces a stack trace if the application fails to catch the error. Inspection of global and local variables, execution of setting breakpoints, arbitrary expressions, stepping through a code one line at one time, and so on are all possible with a source-level debugger. The debugger is developed in Python, demonstrating Python's introspective capabilities. But on the other side, adding a few print declarations to a source code is frequently the fastest method to debug a program: the rapid edit test debug cycle helps make this basic method quite successful.

Chapter 1: Start to learn python

In comparison to other languages like Java, Perl, PHP, and Ruby, Python is a frequently used dynamic programming language. It's also known as the scripting language. It supports automated memory management, numerous programming paradigms, and incorporates object-oriented programming's fundamental notions i.e. OOP.

Python is a highly typed procedural language that comes with a large and comprehensive standard library. Python's library supports a variety of Internet protocols, including FTP and IMAP. It has a distinct grammar that distinguishes it from various programming languages such as C, Java, and C++. Python also has the following outstanding features:

- An open-source language

- A scalable and universal language

- The language is simple and straightforward to learn.

High-level language

It is a common misconception that the programming language's name is inspired by the snake Python. This is not the case. It comes from the title of a renowned television show called Monty Python's Flying Circus.

Python offers a lot of interesting uses. It's commonly utilized in complex content management software like the Django CMS and Plone, as well as frameworks like Django and Pyramid.

1.1 Why should you learn Python?

- Python is a simple language to learn. It has a simple syntax and code that is quite understandable.

- Python has a wide range of uses. It's used for web development, data science, and quick application development, among other things.

- Python is a computer language that enables you to develop programs with minimal lines of program code than many other languages.

- Python's popularity is steadily increasing. It's now one of the most widely used programming languages.

- Python is indeed a cross-platform computer programming language, which means it can operate on a variety of operating systems, including Windows, Mac OS X, Linux, and the Java and.NET virtual machines. It is open-source and free.

- While also Python comes pre-installed on most modern Linux and Mac systems, the version may be outdated. As a result, installing the most recent version is always a smart idea.

Run Python in the Easiest Way

1. The Thonny IDE is the most convenient method to execute Python.

2. The newest version of Python is included in the Thonny IDE. As a result, you will not need to install Python individually.

3. To install Python on your PC, follow the instructions below.

4. Thonny IDE may be downloaded here.

5. To install Thonny on your PC, run the installer.

6. Navigate to File > New. After that, save the file as an a.py file. For instance, hello.py, example.py, and so on.

7. You may name the file anything you like. The file name, however, must finish in. py

8. Fill up the file with Python code and save it.

9. Then choose Run > Run the current script and just press F5.

Install Python personally

Here's how to install and execute Python on the PC, if you do not like to utilize Thonny.

Install the most recent version of Python.

Run the installer and follow the on-screen instructions to install Python.

Check for errors throughout the installation procedure. Python should be included in the environment variables. Python will be added to the environment variables, so you'll be able to execute it from wherever on the machine.

You may also choose the location where Python is downloaded.

You may launch Python when you've completed the installation procedure.

Switch to Immediate mode in Python.

After installing Python, use python on the command line to start an interpreter in the immediate mode. To retrieve the result, we can simply write in Python code and hit Enter.

Enter 1 + 1 then press enter to see what happens. As a result, we obtain 2. You may use this prompt as a calculator. Enter quit() and hit enter to exit this mode.

Use an Integrated Development Environment to run Python (IDE).

To create a Python script file, we may use any text editing program.

All we have to do now is save it with the.py extension. Using an IDE, on the other hand, may make our lives much simpler. For application development, an IDE is a bit of software that gives beneficial capabilities like code suggestions, syntax checking and highlighting file explorers, and so on to the programmer.

Eventually, when people install Python, it comes with an IDE called IDLE. It will allow the user to access Python on any PC. For novices, it's a good IDE.

When you launch IDLE, it launches an interactive Python Shell.

You may now create the new file with the.py extension and save it. Hello.py is a good example.

Fill up the file with Python code and save it. To launch the file, choose Run > Run Module from the menu bar, or just press F5.

1.2 Python's Primary Benefits:

- **Python's success is based on several benefits it delivers to both novices and specialists.**

Python is a simple language to learn and use. The language itself has a small number of features, thus writing your initial applications will take very little time and effort. Python syntax is intended to be simple and easy to understand. Python is an excellent teaching language because of its simplicity, which allows newbies to pick it up fast. As a consequence, developers spend less time worrying about language complexity or understanding code left by others and more time pondering about the issue they're attempting to address.

- **Python is widely used and supported.**

Python is popular and extensively used, as shown by top rankings in surveys including the Tiobe Index and also the vast number of Python-based GitHub projects. Python is compatible with every main platform and operating system as well as the majority of minor ones. Python bindings or wrappers exist for many key libraries and API-powered services, allowing Python to easily interact with them or utilize them directly.

- **Python isn't a "toy" programming language.**

Despite the fact that scripting and automation account for a substantial portion of Python's use cases more on than later, Python is also used to create high-quality software, either as standalone apps or as web services. Python isn't the quickest programming language, but it generates for it in variety.

- **Python continues to progress.**

To stay up with contemporary software development processes, each release of a Python language introduces beneficial new functionality. Coroutines and Asynchronous operations, for example, are now standard elements of a language, making it simpler to develop concurrent Python programs.

What is the purpose of Python?

Python's most fundamental use is as an automation and scripting language. Python isn't only a substitute for batch files or shell scripts; it's also used in tools like Ansible and Salt to handle interactions with application GUIs or web browsers, as well as system provisioning and setup. However, Python's scripting and automation capabilities are only the tips of the iceberg.

Common application programming with Python

Python allows you to construct inter-platform and command-line GUI programs that can be deployed as standalone executables. Although Python does not have the ability to produce a solitary binary from the script, third-party tools such as cx Freeze and PyInstaller may help.

Machine learning and data science with Python

One of Python's most popular use cases is sophisticated data analysis, which has become one of the fastest-growing fields in IT. Python interfaces are found in the great majority of data science and machine learning libraries, making it the most widely used high-level command interface for different numerical methods and machine learning libraries.

RESTful APIs and Web services in Python

Python's third-party web frameworks and native libraries make it easy to build anything from basic REST APIs to full-fledged data-driven websites in a few lines of code. With the correct libraries, Python's newest versions offer significant contributions for asynchronous operations, allowing sites to handle hundreds or even thousands of requests every second

Code generation and metaprogramming in Python

Python treats everything in the language, particularly Python modules and libraries, as an object. This enables Python to operate as a very efficient code generator, allowing developers to create programs that control their functions and provide extensibility that must be difficult or even impossible in other languages.

Python may also be applied to drive code generation technologies like LLVM to produce code in all other languages more effectively.

"Glue language" in Python

Python is known as a "glue language," meaning it can connect unrelated pieces of code usually modules with C language interfaces. In this respect, it is used in machine learning and data science, although that's only one iteration of the overall concept. When you have apps or program domains that you'd want to link but can't communicate with each other directly, Python can help.

How does Python make programming easy?

Python's syntax is designed to be simple and easy to understand. In Python 3.x, a conventional "hello world" is really nothing more than:

```
print("Hello world!")
```

Various syntactical features are available in Python to represent many typical programs flows succinctly. Consider the following example program for lines reading from a text document into the list object while removing each line's closing newline character:

```
with open('myfile.txt') as my_file:
    file_lines = [x.rstrip('\n') for x in my_file]
```

A with or as construction is the context manager that allows you to quickly create one object for the block of code and afterward discard it outside of it. The object in this example is my file, which was created using the open() method. This replaces numerous lines of boilerplate for opening the file, reading specific lines from it, and then closing it.

Another Python quirk is a list comprehension, which is used in the [x... for x in my file] construction. It allows you to iterate over an item that includes other things as in this case, my file and the lines it includes, and every iterated element which is, each x is processed and automatically added to a list.

In Python, you could build a formal for loop just like you would in other languages. The idea is that Python offers a mechanism to describe things such as loops that iterate over several objects and execute a basic action on each element in the loop, as well as working with items that need explicit instantiation and disposal, in a cost-effective manner.

Python programmers may use structures like this to strike a compromise between brevity and readability.

The rest of Python's capabilities are intended to supplement typical use cases. Most recent object types, such as Unicode strings, are incorporated right into the language. Standard-issue data structures include lists, dictionaries (also known as key-value stores or hashmaps, tuples for storing immutable sets of things, and sets for maintaining collections of unique objects.

Python 2 vs. Python 3:

Python is offered in two versions, both of which are enough different to confuse many new users. Python 2.x, an older legacy branch, will be supported i.e., get official upgrades until 2020, after which it may be maintained informally. Many useful and significant features not present in Python 2.x, like additional syntactic features e.g., the walrus operator, stronger concurrency limits, and a more effective interpreter, are available in Python 3.x.

For the longest period, the absence of third-party library support hampered Python 3 uptake. Many Python libraries only supported Python 2, making switching difficult. However, the amount of libraries that solely support Python 2 has decreased in recent years; several of the most prominent libraries now support either Python 2 or Python 3. Python 3 is the best selection for new projects nowadays; you should only use Python 2 if people have no other option. If you're bound with Python 2 version, then please try a few different approaches.

There are no other programming languages that are as simple to use as Python. Other languages are clumsy and difficult to read. If you look at them closely, you'll see that they include a lot of brackets or even words that people won't recognize. It's enough to put someone off who isn't accustomed to programming since all of the terms seem to be scary. Python is a unique language. Besides all the wacky brackets, it uses indentations, resulting in a page that is simpler to read and less cluttered. It employs English instead of words you don't comprehend. The additional special characters have been reduced to a minimal level so that people may glance just at a page of code without feeling overwhelmed. It is one of the most straightforward programming tools available. It looks beautiful on the page and, where possible, will employ a lot of white space to make it simpler to understand what you need to know. If the software is too complicated for you, there are many locations with comments where you may receive an explanation. Overall, it's one of the perfect programming languages for getting ahead or learning the basics of programming. Because this software is written in English, it is quite simple to understand. There aren't many words you won't understand, and you won't have to waste hours trying to find out what its saying. The whole application is in English, and you'll be amazed at how easy it can make things. Python may already be installed on your machine in certain instances. Python will be installed automatically on Mac OS X and Ubuntu PCs. To get started, you'll merely have to download the text interpreter. All you have to do to use Python on a Windows computer is download the program. Python is compatible with all of these programs, even if it isn't installed right away.

People will just use Python on the own at first. It's an excellent program in which to learn and grow. However, you may decide at some point in the future that you want to pursue anything new that Python cannot do on its own. Fortunately, Python can interact with a variety of different programming languages, like JavaScript and C++, so anyone can play around, learn more, and obtain the code you need, even if Python can't do everything. You'll also need to get a text interpreter when you download Python. Python will be able to read your data more easily as a result of this.

You may use basic programs that are often already installed on a computer, like Notepad from Windows, or search for a more user-friendly interpreter. After you've decided on an interpreter to use, it's time to start creating code. Some people who are inexperienced in coding may be concerned about getting the code to function. Another place where Python can help is in this area. It might be capable of taking the words people are typing and, with the aid of the translator, throw them back out in a matter of seconds. While you're working on it, people can test what they are doing! There are several advantages to utilizing the Python software. Beginners will appreciate how accessible this program is and how quickly they can pick up on some of the basic commands. Even experienced programmers will be blown away by how well this all comes together!

Python is mostly used for:

- Web design and development

- System utilities i.e. command-line programs and system admin tools

- User Interfaces in Graphics like in Tkinter, Qt, gtk

- Embedded scripting

- Scripting on the internet

- Database programming and access

- Prototyping and development in a short amount of time

- Programming for games

Programming in a distributed environment

Chapter 2: Python variables

The variable is a designated place in memory where data is stored. Variables may be thought of as a container for data that may be altered later in the program. Variables are storage containers for data values. As an example, we've established a variable called number in this case. The variable has been given the value of ten.

```
number = 10
```

Variables may be compared to a bag in which books may be stored and changed at any moment.

```
number = 10
number = 1.1
```

The initial value of the number was ten. It was afterward updated to 1.1.

Creating a variable entails the following steps:

It is not feasible to declare a new variable in Python using a command. A variable is considered to be established when you first assign a value to it. Variables don't have to be allocated to a specific class, and they may change types after they've been established.

Variable Casting:

Casting can be used to specify a variable's data type.

Get the type:

The type() function returns a variable's data type.

Use single or double quotes?

String variables may be declared with single and double quotations.

A sensitive case:

The variables' names are case-sensitive.

2.1 Variables Names

A variable's name might be short, like x and y or it may be lengthy, like class, book name, or total inches.

Variables in Python have the following rules:

- A variable's name must begin with an underscore character or a letter.

- The initial character in any variable name cannot be a number.

- In variable names, both underscore like A-z, _, 0-9, and alphanumeric letters are used.

- Whenever it concerns variable titles, case matters: class, Class, and CLASS represent three different variables.

- Lowercase alphabets i.e. a to z or capital alphabets i.e. A to Z characters, numerals i.e. 0 to 9, and an underscore (_) should be used in variable names.

- Make a name for yourself that makes sense.

- If you wish to make a variable name with two words, separate them with an underscore.

- To declare a constant, use capital letters wherever feasible.

- Never use special characters such as !, @, #, $, percent, and so on.

- A digit should not be used to begin the name of a variable.

Variable Names with More Than One Word (Multi words):

Interpreting variable names with more than one word might be difficult.

You may make them easier to read in many ways:

Camel case:

Each phrase, except for the first, starts with a capital letter.

myVariableName = "Ali"

Pascal case:

Each word's initial letter is capitalized.

MyVariableName = "Ali"

Snake case:

Each word is separated by an underscore character.

my_variable_name = "Ali"

2.2 Organize/Unpack a Collection:

You may use this technique if you have an integer, tuple, or another group of values. Python facilitates the removal of values and the storage of those values in variables. Unpacking is the term for this process.

2.3 Output variables

In Python, the print expression is often used to produce values.

When text and a variable are combined, a + character is used.

The + sign may also be used to link any variable to the preceding variable.

For numbers, the + character acts as a logical operator. If you try to combine numbers and strings in Python, you may get an error.

2.4 Variables at a Global Level:

Variables that are produced beyond a function are known as global variables. Global variables should be used by everyone, both inside and outside of methods.

If you create a variable with the same name inside a feature, it will be local, which means it will only exist inside that function. The same-named global variable would remain global or have a similar meaning as before.

The global keywords:

A variable generated inside a feature is generally local, implying it can always be retrieved inside that function.

Within a function, a global keyword can be used to create a global variable.

The global keyword is used to change a global variable inside a function.

Assigning values to Variables in Python

As you can see from the preceding example, you will use an assignment operator = to allocate a value to a variable in Python.

Example 1: Declaring and assigning value to a variable

```
website = "apple.com"
print(website)
```

Output:

The variable website was given the value apple.com in the above program. The value allocated to the website, i.e. apple.com, was then printed out.

```
apple.com
```

Example 2: Changing the value of a variable

```
website = "apple.com"
print(website)

# assigning a new value to website
website = "programiz.com"

print(website)
```

Output:

```
apple.com
programiz.com
```

Initially, its website variable in the above program was set to apple.com. After that, the value is set to programiz.com.

Example 3: Assigning multiple values to multiple variables

We may accomplish this as follows if we wish to set the identical value to numerous variables at the same time:

```
a, b, c = 5, 3.2, "Hello"

print (a)
print (b)
print (c)
```

In the second program, the 3 variables x, y, and z are all given the identical string.

```
x = y = z = "same"

print (x)
print (y)
print (z)
```

2.5 Constants

The constant is a sort of variable that has a fixed value. Constants may be thought of as containers that carry information that cannot be modified later.

Constants might be thought of as a bag in which to keep certain books that cannot be replaced once put inside.

Assigning value to constant in Python

Constants are commonly defined and allocated in a module in Python. The module is a new file that contains variables, functions, and other information that is imported into the main file. Constants are typed in all upper case letters inside the module, with underscores between the terms.

Example 3: Declaring and assigning value to a constant

Create a constant.py:

```
PI = 3.14
GRAVITY = 9.8
```

Create a main.py:

```
import constant

print(constant.PI)
print(constant.GRAVITY)
```

Output:

```
3.14
9.8
```

We build a constant.py module directory in the preceding application. The constant value is then assigned to PI and GRAVITY. The constant module is then imported and a main.py file is created. Finally, the constant value is printed.

Chapter 3: Machine learning

Machine Learning is the process of teaching a computer to learn from data and statistics.

Machine Learning is the first step toward artificial intelligence (AI).

Software that evaluates data and attempts to anticipate the result is known as machine learning.

Set of data

A data set is actually the collection of data in a computer's thinking. It might be everything from a simple array to a whole database.

An array may be shown as follows:

```
[99,86,87,88,111,86,103,87,94,78,77,85,86]
```

The following is an example of the database:

Carname	Color	Age	Speed	AutoPass
BMW	red	5	99	Y
Volvo	black	7	86	Y
VW	gray	8	87	N
VW	white	7	88	Y
Ford	white	2	111	Y
VW	white	17	86	Y
Tesla	red	2	103	Y
BMW	black	9	87	Y
Volvo	gray	4	94	N
Ford	white	11	78	N
Toyota	gray	12	77	N
VW	white	9	85	N
Toyota	blue	6	86	Y

We can assume that the average number is approximately 80 or 90 by checking at the array, and we can also figure out the greatest and lowest values, but what more can we do?

And we can see from the information that white is the most frequent color and the oldest vehicle is 17 years old, so what if we can determine if a vehicle had an AutoPass just by checking through the other values?

That is the purpose of Machine Learning! Analyzing data and making predictions!

Types of Data

It's crucial to understand what kind of data we're working with before we can evaluate it.

The data types may be divided into three categories:

- Numerical
- Categorical
- Ordinal

Numerical:

Numbers are numerical data, which may be divided into two numeric categories:

1. Data That Isn't Continuous (Discrete Data)

The numbers can only be expressed as integers. The number of automobiles going past, for example.

2. Data that is constantly updated (Continuous Data)

The integers with an unlimited number of possibilities. For instance, the cost of an item and the size of the item

Categorical:

Categorical data is a set of values which cannot be compared to one another. A color value, for example, or any no/yes values.

Ordinal:

Ordinal data are similar to categorical data, but they may be compared. For instance, at school, an A is preferable to a B, and so on.

Knowing what sort of data your data source contains can help you choose which methodology to apply while studying it.

3.1 Mean, Median, and Mode

What can we understand from a group of digits/numbers?

There are three values that we are interested in when it comes to Machine Learning (and in mathematics):

Mean - The average value

Median - The midpoint value

Mode - The most common value

For instance, we've recorded the following speeds for 13 vehicles:

```
speed = [99,86,87,88,111,86,103,87,94,78,77,85,86]
```

What is the speed's average, median, or most common value?

Mean

The mean value is called the average value.

To obtain the mean, add all of the values together and divide by several values:

```
(99+86+87+88+111+86+103+87+94+78+77+85+86) / 13 = 89.77
```

As an example:

To obtain the average speed, use a NumPy mean() method:

```
import numpy

speed = [99,86,87,88,111,86,103,87,94,78,77,85,86]

x = numpy.mean(speed)

print(x)
```

Median

After you've sorted all of the data, a median value is one value in the middle:

Before you can determine the median, you must first sort the data.

77, 78, 85, 86, 86, 86, **87**, 87, 88, 94, 99, 103, 111

As an example:

```
import numpy

speed = [99,86,87,88,111,86,103,87,94,78,77,85,86]

x = numpy.median(speed)

print(x)
```

To determine the center value, use a NumPy median() method:

Divide the total of the numbers in middle by two since there are two numbers in the center.

$$77, 78, 85, 86, 86, \underline{86, 87}, 87, 94, 98, 99, 103$$

$$(86 + 87) / 2 = \underline{86.5}$$

As an example:

Using a NumPy module:

```
import numpy

speed = [99,86,87,88,86,103,87,94,78,77,85,86]

x = numpy.median(speed)

print(x)
```

Mode

The value that occurs the most times is called the Mode value:

$$99, \underline{86}, 87, 88, 111, \underline{86}, 103, 87, 94, 78, 77, 85, \underline{86} = 86$$

As an example:

To discover the number that occurs the most, use a SciPy mode() method:

```
from scipy import stats

speed = [99,86,87,88,111,86,103,87,94,78,77,85,86]

x = stats.mode(speed)

print(x)
```

Each Mean, Median, and Mode are approaches that are frequently used in Machine Learning, therefore understanding the notion behind them is essential.

What is Standard Deviation?

The standard deviation is simply a number that expresses how far the data are spread out.

The low standard deviation indicates that the majority of the data points are near to the mean (average).

The numbers are spread out across a larger range when the standard deviation is high.

Consider the following scenario:

This time, we recorded the speeds of seven vehicles:

```
speed = [86,87,88,86,87,85,86]
```

A standard deviation is the following:

```
0.9
```

Meaning that the majority of values are within 0.9 of the mean value of 86.4.

Let's try the same thing with a broader range of numbers:

```
speed = [32,111,138,28,59,77,97]
```

A standard deviation is the following:

37.85

Meaning that the majority of values are within 37.85 of the mean value of 77.4.

As you can see, a greater standard deviation means the numbers are spread out across a larger range.

The standard deviation may be calculated using the NumPy module:

As an example:

To calculate the standard deviation, use a NumPy std() method:

```
import numpy

speed = [86,87,88,86,87,85,86]

x = numpy.std(speed)

print(x)
```

As an example:

Example:

```
import numpy

speed = [32,111,138,28,59,77,97]

x = numpy.std(speed)

print(x)
```

3.2 Variance

Another statistic that illustrates how evenly distributed the numbers are is variance.

In reality, the standard deviation may be calculated by taking a square root of a variance!

Alternatively, you may obtain the variance by multiplying a standard deviation by itself!

To determine the variance, perform these steps:

1. Calculate the mean.

$$(32+111+138+28+59+77+97) \; / \; 7 = 77.4$$

2. Calculate the difference from the mean for each value.

$$
\begin{aligned}
32 - 77.4 &= -45.4 \\
111 - 77.4 &= 33.6 \\
138 - 77.4 &= 60.6 \\
28 - 77.4 &= -49.4 \\
59 - 77.4 &= -18.4 \\
77 - 77.4 &= -0.4 \\
97 - 77.4 &= 19.6
\end{aligned}
$$

3. Determine the square value for each difference.

$$(-45.4)^2 = 2061.16$$
$$(33.6)^2 = 1128.96$$
$$(60.6)^2 = 3672.36$$
$$(-49.4)^2 = 2440.36$$
$$(-18.4)^2 = 338.56$$
$$(-0.4)^2 = 0.16$$
$$(19.6)^2 = 384.16$$

4. An average number of such squared differences in the variance.

```
(2061.16+1128.96+3672.36+2440.36+338.56+0.16+384.16) / 7 = 1432.2
```

Fortunately, NumPy has such a method for calculating variance:

As an example:

```
import numpy

speed = [32,111,138,28,59,77,97]

x = numpy.var(speed)

print(x)
```

To get the variance, use a NumPy var() method:

3.3 Standard Deviation

As we've seen, each standard deviation is calculated by taking a square root of a variance:

$$\sqrt{1432.25} = 37.85$$

Use NumPy to compute the standard deviation, as in the previous example:

As an example:

To calculate the standard deviation, use a NumPy std() method:

```
import numpy

speed = [32,111,138,28,59,77,97]

x = numpy.std(speed)

print(x)
```

Symbols

The symbol Sigma σ is often used to denote standard deviation.

A symbol Sigma Square σ2 is often used to denote variance.

3.4 What Are Percentiles?

Percentiles are numbers for use in statistics to represent the value that a certain percent of values are less than.

Consider the following scenario: Let's imagine we have a list of all the ages of everyone who lives on a street.

```
ages = [5,31,43,48,50,41,7,11,15,39,80,82,32,2,8,6,25,36,27,61,31]
```

What percentage of the population is in the 75th percentile? The result is 43, indicating that 75percent of the total of population is aged 43 or younger.

A method for getting the given percentile is available in the NumPy module:

As an Example:

To get the percentiles, use a NumPy percentile() method:

```
import numpy

ages = [5,31,43,48,50,41,7,11,15,39,80,82,32,2,8,6,25,36,27,61,31]

x = numpy.percentile(ages, 75)

print(x)
```

As an Example:

And what's the age at which 90% of the population is younger?

```
import numpy

ages = [5,31,43,48,50,41,7,11,15,39,80,82,32,2,8,6,25,36,27,61,31]

x = numpy.percentile(ages, 90)

print(x)
```

3.5 Data Distribution

We used extremely tiny amounts of information in our examples earlier in this course to help us comprehend the various concepts.

The data sets in the actual world are substantially larger, yet gathering real data of the world, at least at the beginning of a project, may be challenging.

How do we obtain big data sets?

We utilize the Python package NumPy to generate large data sets in testing, which has a variety of techniques for generating random data sets of arbitrary size.

Example:

Make an array of 250 random floats in the range of 0 to 5:

```
import numpy

x = numpy.random.uniform(0.0, 5.0, 250)

print(x)
```

Histogram:

We can use the data we obtained to create a histogram to display the data set.

To create a histogram, we'll utilize the Python program Matplotlib.

Example

Create/Draw a histogram:

```
import numpy
import matplotlib.pyplot as plt

x = numpy.random.uniform(0.0, 5.0, 250)

plt.hist(x, 5)
plt.show()
```

Answer:

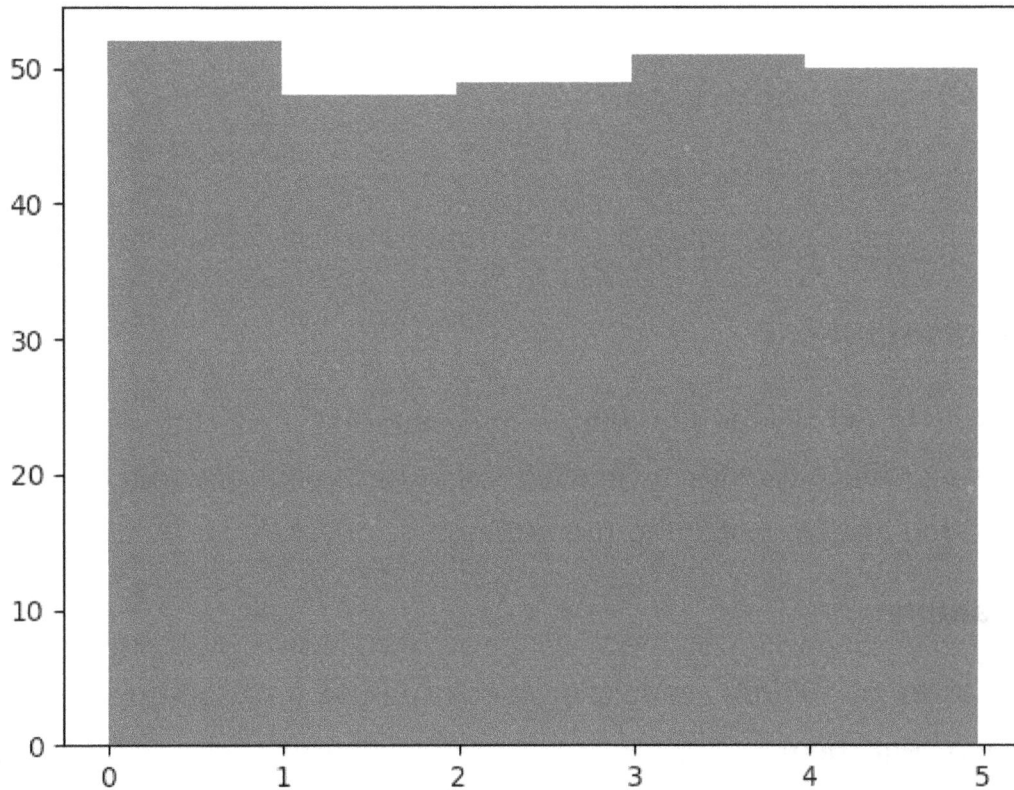

Histogram Explaination:

We create a histogram having 5 bars using an array from the previous example.

The first bar indicates the number of items in the array that are within 0 and 1.

The second bar depicts the number of values that fall within 1 and 2.

And so forth.

As a consequence, we get the following:

There are 52 values within 0 and 1

There are 48 values within 1 and 2

There are 49 values within 2 and 3

There are 51 values within 3 and 4

There are 50 values within 4 and 5

Big Data Distributions

Although a data set of 250 numbers is not regarded as large, now that you know how to produce a random collection of values, you may make a data set as large as you like by modifying the settings.

As an example:

Create an array of 100000 random integers and use a histogram having 100 bars to represent them:

```
import numpy
import matplotlib.pyplot as plt

x = numpy.random.uniform(0.0, 5.0, 100000)

plt.hist(x, 100)
plt.show()
```

3.6 Normal Data Distribution

We learned how to create a random array of a certain size and between two specified values in the previous chapter.

We'll learn how to make an array with values centered around a single item in this chapter.

This type of data distribution is known in probability theory as the Gaussian data distribution or the normal data distribution, just after mathematician Carl Friedrich Gauss, who devised the formula for it.

As an example:

A basic normal data distribution looks like this:

```
import numpy
import matplotlib.pyplot as plt

x = numpy.random.normal(5.0, 1.0, 100000)

plt.hist(x, 100)
plt.show()
```

Result:

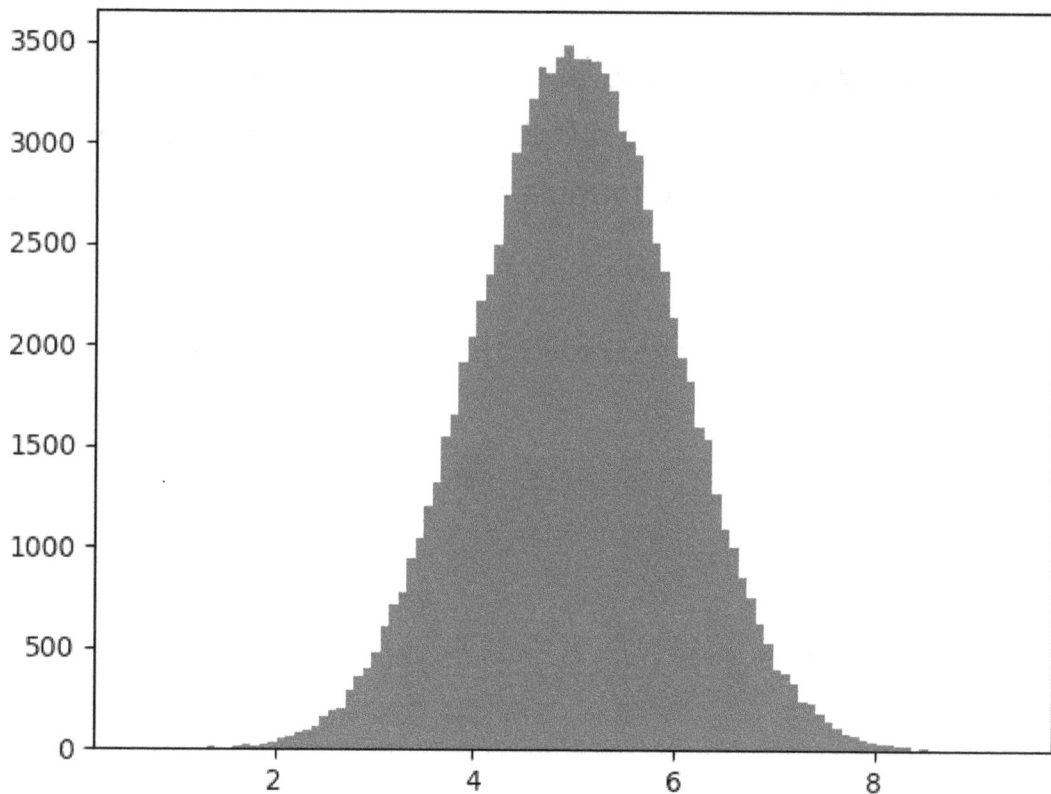

Histogram Explaination:

To construct a histogram with 100 bars, we utilize the array returned by the numpy.random.normal() function, which has 100000 values.

The mean value is set to 5.0, while a standard deviation is set to 1.0.

This means that the results should be clustered around 5.0 and seldom deviate from the mean by more than 1.0.

As you can observe from the histogram, the majority of the values are somewhere within 4.0 and 6.0, with a peak around 5.0.

3.7 Scatter Plot

The scatter plot is a graph in which each data point is symbolized by a dot.

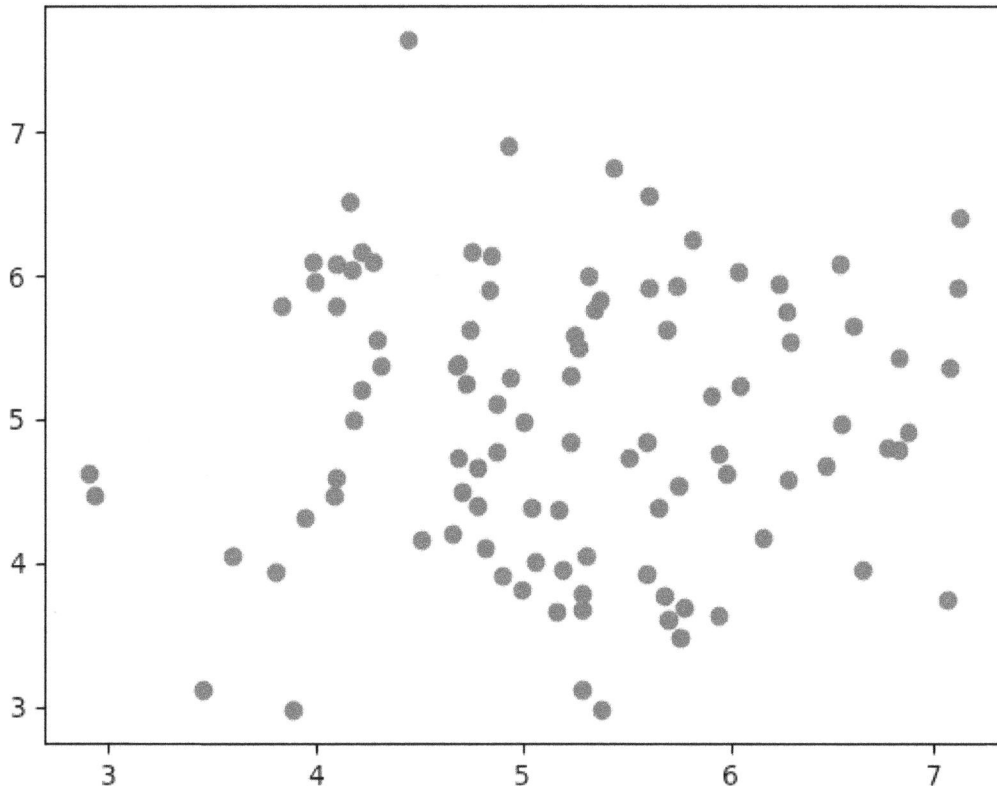

The Matplotlib module offers a method for producing scatter plots that require two identical-length arrays, one for the x-axis values and the other for the y-axis data:

```
x = [5,7,8,7,2,17,2,9,4,11,12,9,6]

y = [99,86,87,88,111,86,103,87,94,78,77,85,86]
```

Each car's age is represented by the x array.

Each car's speed is represented by the y array.

Example:

To create a scatter plot diagram, use the scatter() method:

```
import matplotlib.pyplot as plt

x = [5,7,8,7,2,17,2,9,4,11,12,9,6]
y = [99,86,87,88,111,86,103,87,94,78,77,85,86]

plt.scatter(x, y)
plt.show()
```

Result:

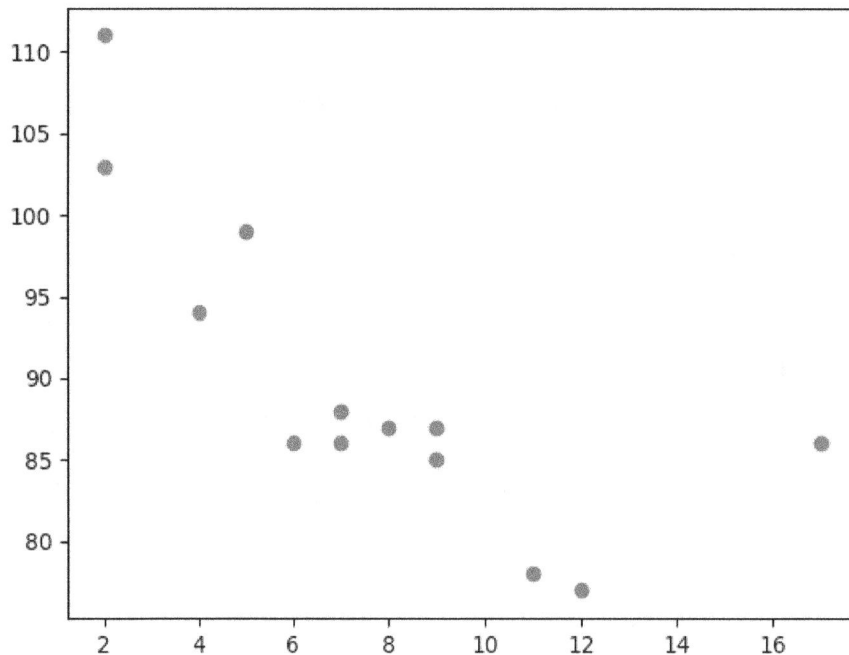

Scatter Plot Explanation:

The ages are shown on the x-axis, while the speeds are shown on the y-axis.

The graphic shows that the two quickest automobiles were both two years old, while the slowest vehicle was twelve years old.

3.8 Random Data Distributions

The data sets in Machine Learning may include hundreds, if not millions, of variables.

When assessing an algorithm, you may need to utilize randomly generated values if you don't have real-world data.

The NumPy module may assist us with that, as we learned in the last chapter!

Let's make two arrays, each containing 1000 random integers drawn from a normal distribution of data.

The mean of the first array will be fixed to 5.0, with a standard deviation of 1.0.

The mean of the second array will be set to 10.0, with the standard deviation of 2.0:

Example:

The scatter plot having 1000 dots:

```
import numpy
import matplotlib.pyplot as plt

x = numpy.random.normal(5.0, 1.0, 1000)
y = numpy.random.normal(10.0, 2.0, 1000)

plt.scatter(x, y)
plt.show()
```

Result:

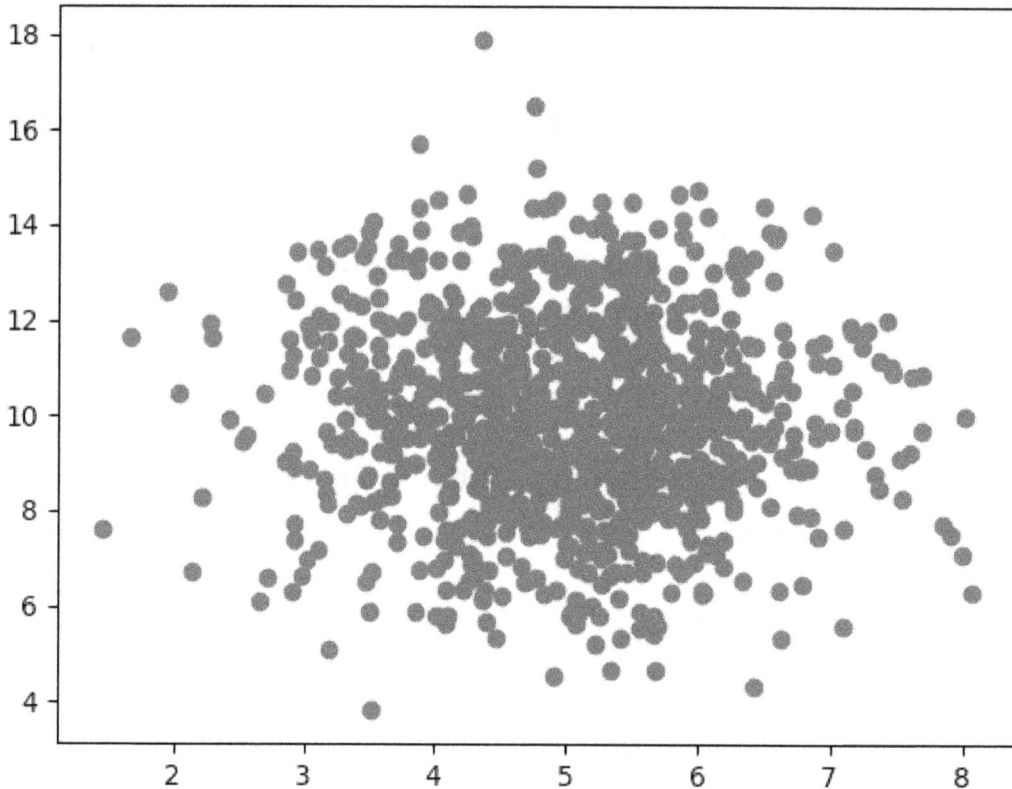

Scatter Plot Explanation:

On the x-axis, all dots seem concentrated around a value of 5; on the y-axis, each dot seem concentrated around a value of 10.

On the y-axis, we can also observe that the dispersion is larger than that on the x-axis.

Regression

When attempting to determine the connection between variables, the word regression is utilized.

That connection is applied to determine the outcome of upcoming occurrences in Machine Learning and statistical modeling.

3.9 Linear Regression

Linear regression draws a straight line across all of the data points based on their connection.

This line may be used to forecast values in the future.

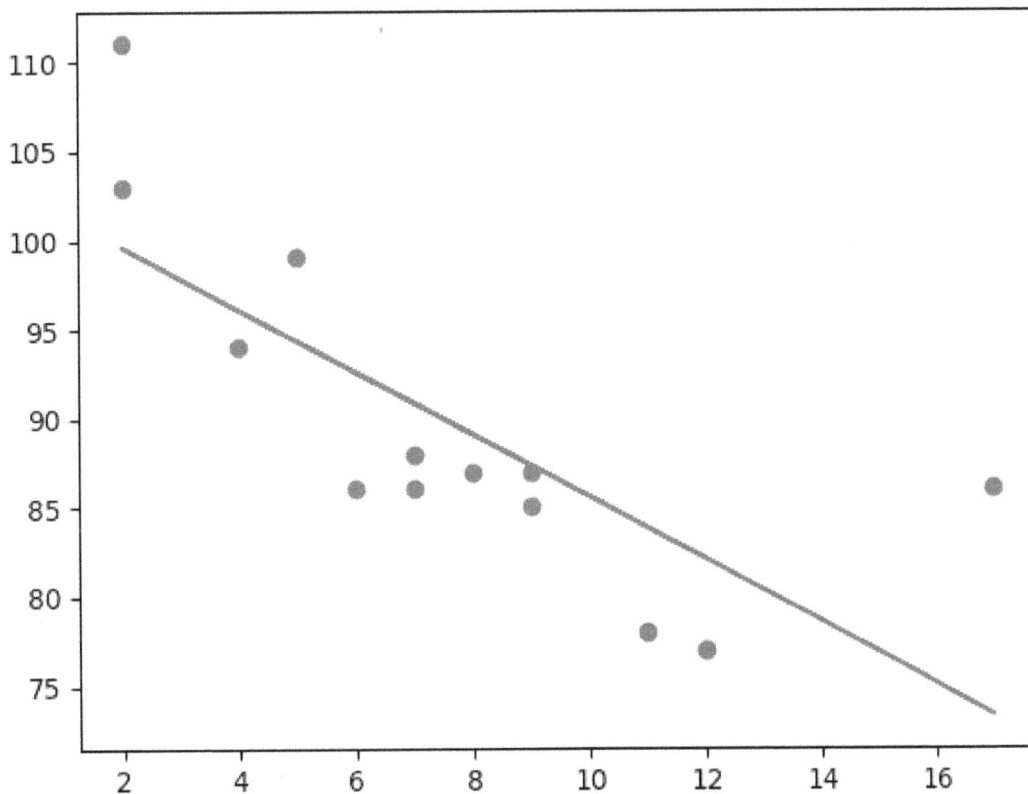

Predicting the next is crucial in Machine Learning.

Working of linear regression?

Python has functions for determining a link between data points and drawing a linear regression line. Instead of going over the mathematical formula, we'll teach you how to apply these strategies.

The x-axis indicates age, while the y-axis indicates the speed in the example below. We recorded the speed and age13 vehicles as they passed through a tollbooth. Let's see whether we can utilize the data we gathered inside a linear regression:

Example:

To begin, create a scatter plot as follows:

```
import matplotlib.pyplot as plt

x = [5,7,8,7,2,17,2,9,4,11,12,9,6]
y = [99,86,87,88,111,86,103,87,94,78,77,85,86]

plt.scatter(x, y)
plt.show()
```

Result:

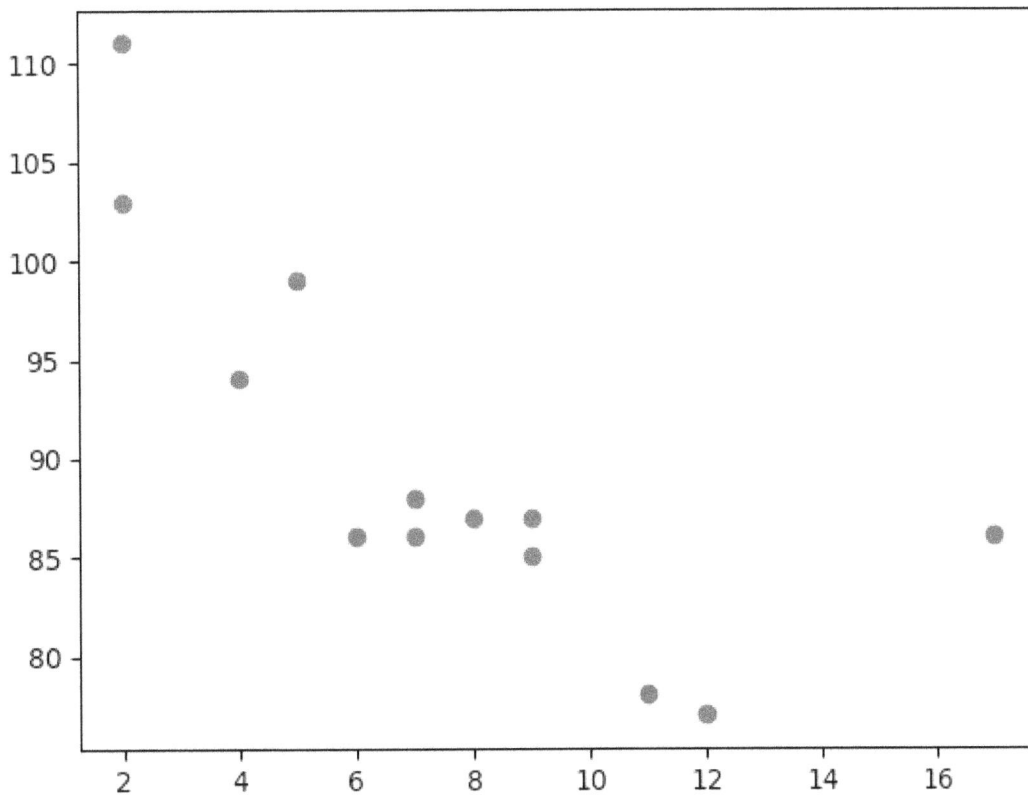

Example:

Import scipy and construct a Linear Regression line:

```
import matplotlib.pyplot as plt
from scipy import stats

x = [5,7,8,7,2,17,2,9,4,11,12,9,6]
y = [99,86,87,88,111,86,103,87,94,78,77,85,86]

slope, intercept, r, p, std_err = stats.linregress(x, y)

def myfunc(x):
  return slope * x + intercept

mymodel = list(map(myfunc, x))

plt.scatter(x, y)
plt.plot(x, mymodel)
plt.show()
```

Result:

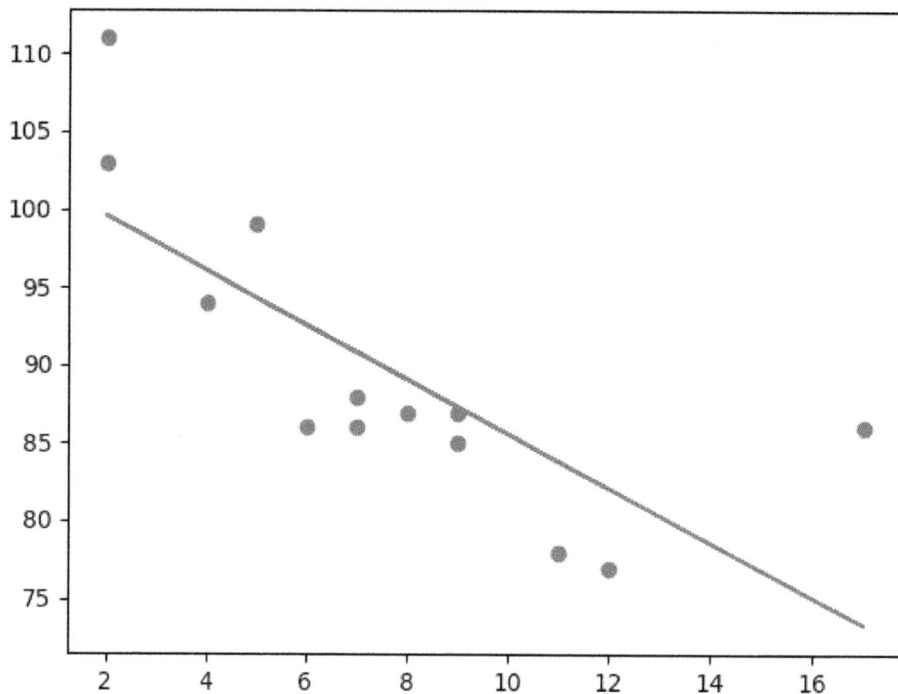

Example Explaination:

Import the modules that you need.

```
import matplotlib.pyplot as plt
from scipy import stats
```

Make the following arrays to represent the y and x axis values:

```
x = [5,7,8,7,2,17,2,9,4,11,12,9,6]
y = [99,86,87,88,111,86,103,87,94,78,77,85,86]
```

Run the method that returns certain critical Linear Regression key values:

```
slope, intercept, r, p, std_err = stats.linregress(x, y)
```

Initialize a function that returns a new value based on the intercept and slope variables. This new value indicates where the relevant x value will now be put on the y-axis:

```
def myfunc(x):
    return slope * x + intercept
```

Run the function on each value in the x array. As a consequence, a unique array with new y-axis values will be created:

```
mymodel = list(map(myfunc, x))
```

Create an original scatter plot as follows:

```
plt.scatter(x, y)
```

Draw the linear regression line as follows:

```
plt.plot(x, mymodel)
```

Display the diagram as follows:

```
plt.show()
```

R stands for Relationship

It's crucial to understand the link between the values on the y-axis and the values on the x-axis; if there isn't one; linear regression won't be able to predict anything.

The coefficient of correlation, or r, is the name given to this connection.

An r value ranges between -1 to 1, with 0 indicating no association and 1 and -1 indicating 100% association.

Simply you have to do is supply the x and y numbers to the Scipy and Python module, and it will calculate the result for you.

Example:

In a linear regression, how effectively does my data fit?

```
from scipy import stats

x = [5,7,8,7,2,17,2,9,4,11,12,9,6]
y = [99,86,87,88,111,86,103,87,94,78,77,85,86]

slope, intercept, r, p, std_err = stats.linregress(x, y)

print(r)
```

Predict Future Values

We can now utilize the data we've obtained to forecast future values.

Example: Let's say you're trying to forecast the overall speed of a ten-year-old automobile.

To accomplish so, we'll use the same myfunc() method as in the previous example:

```
def myfunc(x):
    return slope * x + intercept
```

Example:

Estimate the approximate speed of a ten-year-old automobile:

```
from scipy import stats

x = [5,7,8,7,2,17,2,9,4,11,12,9,6]
y = [99,86,87,88,111,86,103,87,94,78,77,85,86]

slope, intercept, r, p, std_err = stats.linregress(x, y)

def myfunc(x):
    return slope * x + intercept

speed = myfunc(10)

print(speed)
```

The example projected an 85.6 mph speed, which we could also see in the diagram:

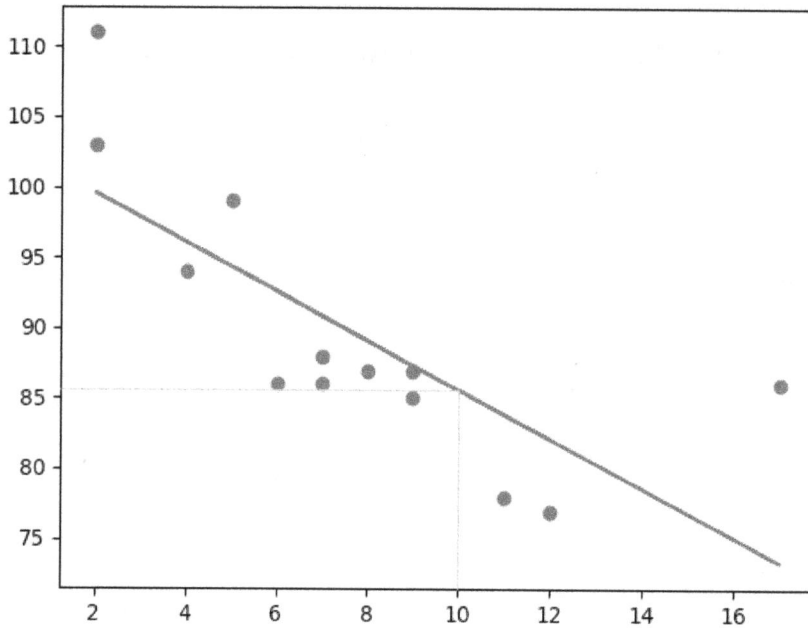

Bad Fit?

Let's imagine a situation where linear regression isn't the optimal strategy for predicting future values.

Example:

These x- and y-axis values should lead to a poor fit for linear regression:

```
import matplotlib.pyplot as plt
from scipy import stats

x = [89,43,36,36,95,10,66,34,38,20,26,29,48,64,6,5,36,66,72,40]
y = [21,46,3,35,67,95,53,72,58,10,26,34,90,33,38,20,56,2,47,15]

slope, intercept, r, p, std_err = stats.linregress(x, y)

def myfunc(x):
  return slope * x + intercept

mymodel = list(map(myfunc, x))

plt.scatter(x, y)
plt.plot(x, mymodel)
plt.show()
```

Result:

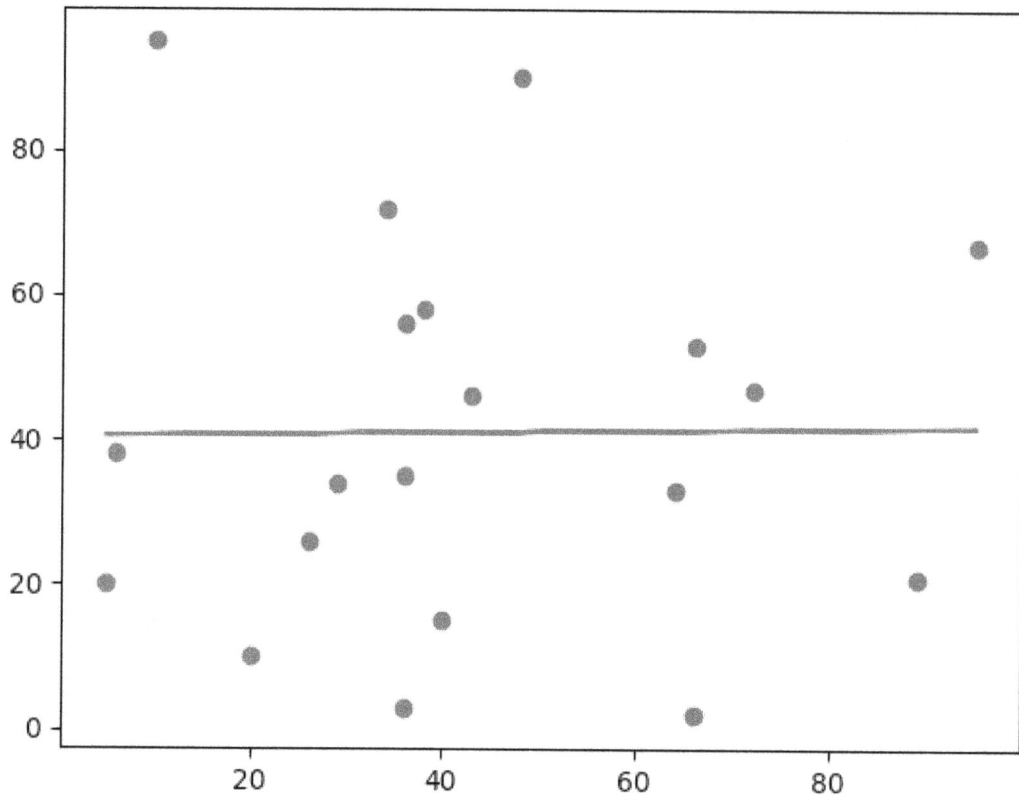

And what about the r in a relationship?

Example:

The r value should be quite low.

```python
import numpy
from scipy import stats

x = [89,43,36,36,95,10,66,34,38,20,26,29,48,64,6,5,36,66,72,40]
y = [21,46,3,35,67,95,53,72,58,10,26,34,90,33,38,20,56,2,47,15]

slope, intercept, r, p, std_err = stats.linregress(x, y)

print(r)
```

The result: 0.013 denotes a poor association and suggests that this data set is unsuitable for linear regression.

3.10 Polynomial Regression

If your data points do not match the linear regression which is a straight line connecting all data points), polynomial regression may be the best option.

Polynomial regression, similar to linear regression, looks for the optimum method to draw a line across the data points based on the connection among the variables x and y.

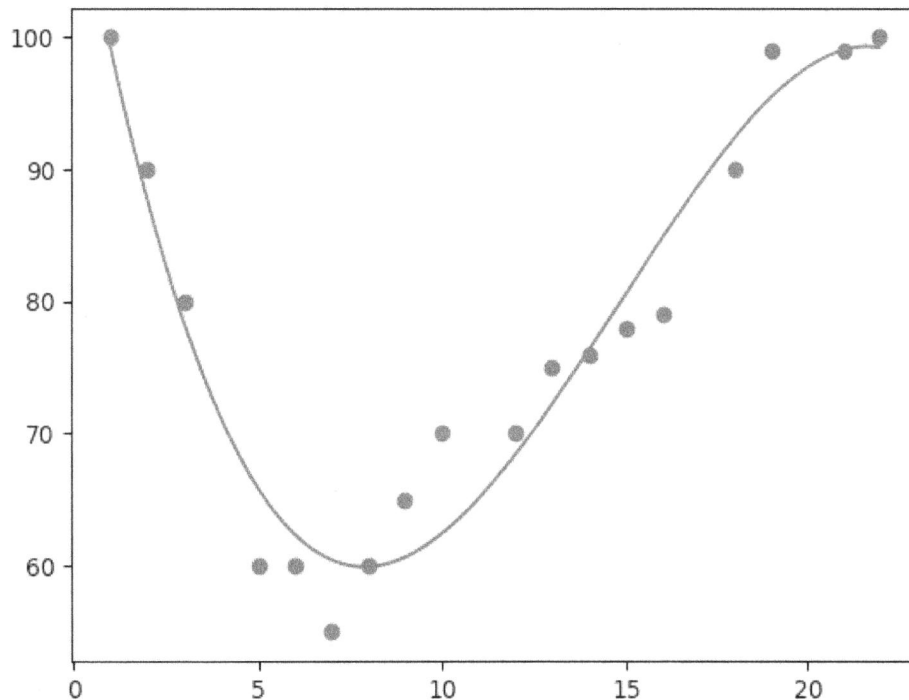

Working of polynomial regression:

Python has functions for determining a link between data points and drawing a polynomial regression line. Instead of going over the mathematical formula, we'll teach you how to apply these strategies.

In the example below, 18 automobiles were recorded as they passed through a tollbooth.

We recorded the car's speed as well as a time of day hour when it passed us.

All hours of a day are shown on the x-axis, while the speed is shown on the y-axis:

Example:

To begin, create a scatter plot as follows:

```
import matplotlib.pyplot as plt

x = [1,2,3,5,6,7,8,9,10,12,13,14,15,16,18,19,21,22]
y = [100,90,80,60,60,55,60,65,70,70,75,76,78,79,90,99,99,100]

plt.scatter(x, y)
plt.show()
```

Result:

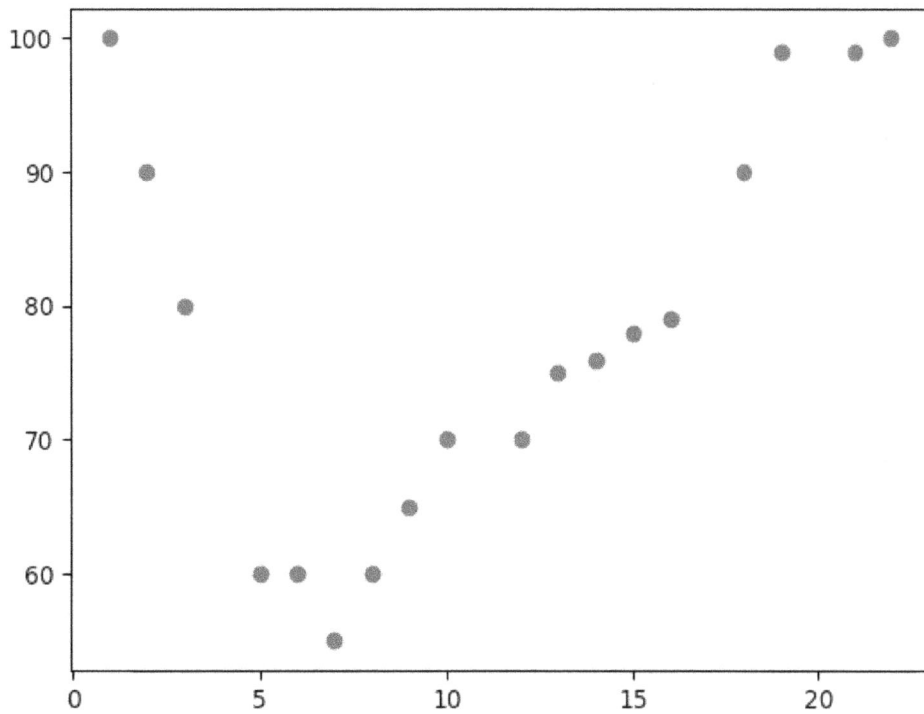

Example:

Import numpy and matplotlib, then draw the Polynomial Regression line as follows:

```
import numpy
import matplotlib.pyplot as plt

x = [1,2,3,5,6,7,8,9,10,12,13,14,15,16,18,19,21,22]
y = [100,90,80,60,60,55,60,65,70,70,75,76,78,79,90,99,99,100]

mymodel = numpy.poly1d(numpy.polyfit(x, y, 3))

myline = numpy.linspace(1, 22, 100)

plt.scatter(x, y)
plt.plot(myline, mymodel(myline))
plt.show()
```

Result:

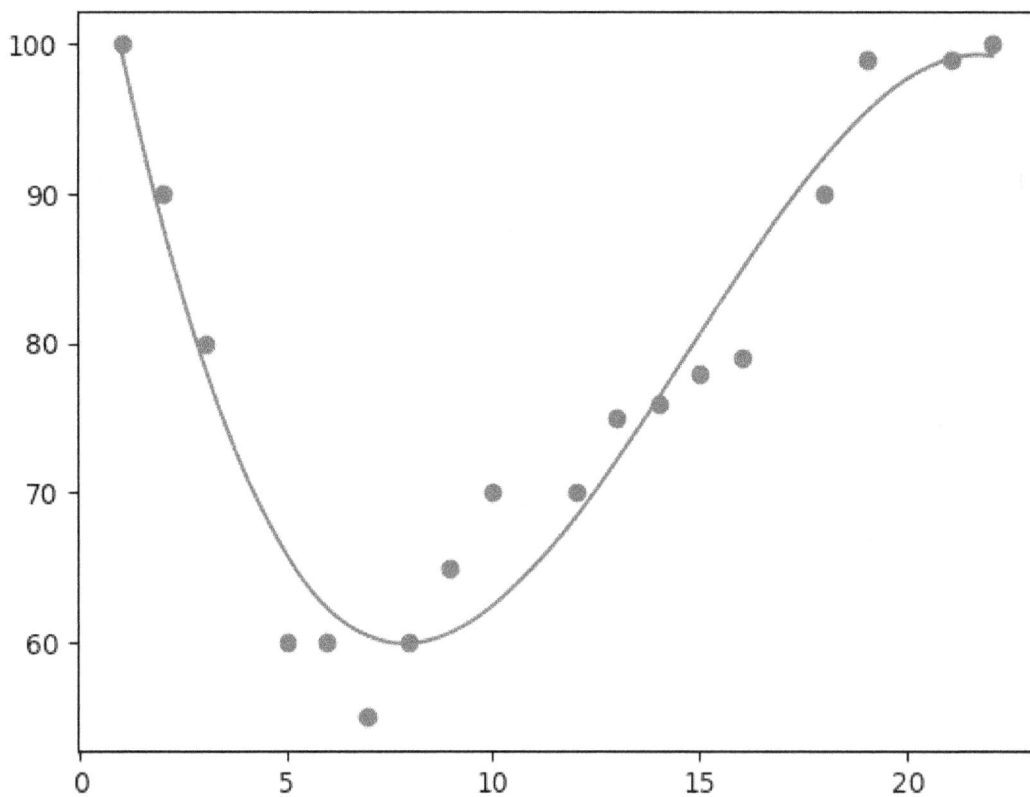

R-Squared

It is critical to understand how strongly the x- and y-axis values are related; if there is no link, polynomial regression cannot be utilized to forecast anything.

The r-squared number is used to assess the connection.

The r-squared value varies from 0 to 1, with 0 indicating no association and 1 indicating 100% connection.

This value will be computed for you by Python using the Sklearn module; all you must do is provide it the y and x arrays:

Example:

In a polynomial regression, how well does my data fit?

```
import numpy
from sklearn.metrics import r2_score

x = [1,2,3,5,6,7,8,9,10,12,13,14,15,16,18,19,21,22]
y = [100,90,80,60,60,55,60,65,70,70,75,76,78,79,90,99,99,100]

mymodel = numpy.poly1d(numpy.polyfit(x, y, 3))

print(r2_score(y, mymodel(x)))
```

Note: The 0.94 indicates that the association is quite strong, and we may utilize polynomial regression to make future predictions.

3.11 Multiple Regression

Multiple regression is similar to linear regression, but it includes upwards of one independent value, implying that we are attempting to predict a value using two or more factors.

We can forecast a car's CO2 emissions based on its engine size, but multiple regression allows us to include extra factors, such as the car's weight, to improve the accuracy of the forecast.

Working of multiple regression:

We have modules in Python that will perform the job for us. To begin, import the Pandas module.

We can scan csv files then return the DataFrame object using the Pandas module.

After that, build a list of independent values and label it X.

Create a variable named y to hold the dependent values.

Each list of independent variables is usually labeled with an upper case X, while a list of dependant values is labeled with a lower case y.

We'll need to import the sklearn module since we'll be using several of its methods.

To generate a linear regression object, we'll utilize the LinearRegression() function from the sklearn package.

Fit() is a method on this object that accepts as input all dependant and independent values then fills a regression object with data that specifies the connection.

We now have the regression object that can forecast CO2 levels based on the weight and volume of an automobile.

Example:

To see the entire example in action, go to:

```
import pandas
from sklearn import linear_model

df = pandas.read_csv("cars.csv")

X = df[['Weight', 'Volume']]
y = df['CO2']

regr = linear_model.LinearRegression()
regr.fit(X, y)

#predict the CO2 emission of a car where the weight is 2300kg, and the volume is 1300cm³:
predictedCO2 = regr.predict([[2300, 1300]])

print(predictedCO2)
```

Result:

```
[107.2087328]
```

An automobile with a 1.3 liter engine and a weight of 2300 kg would emit roughly 107 grams of CO2 each kilometer driven, according to our calculations.

Coefficient

A coefficient is a number that represents the connection between two variables that are unknown.

Example: Assuming x is the variable, 2x is x multiplied by two. The number 2 represents the coefficient, while x is an unknown variable. In this scenario, we may inquire about the weight-to-CO2 coefficient and the volume-to-CO2 coefficient. The answer(s) we obtain inform us what will happen if either of the independent quantities is increased or decreased.

Example:

Print the regression object's coefficient values:

```python
import pandas
from sklearn import linear_model

df = pandas.read_csv("cars.csv")

X = df[['Weight', 'Volume']]
y = df['CO2']

regr = linear_model.LinearRegression()
regr.fit(X, y)

print(regr.coef_)
```

Result:

```
[0.00755095 0.00780526]
```

3.12 Scale

Scale Features:

It might be challenging to compare data that has various values and even various measuring units. What is the difference between kilos and meters? Or how about altitude vs. time?

Scaling is the solution to this issue. We may change the size of the data to make it simpler to compare.

Comparing the volume 1.0 to the weight 790 might be tough, although if we scale those all into similar numbers, we can observe how much one number differs from the other.

Scaling data may be done in a variety of ways; in this lesson, we'll utilize a technique called standardization.

This formula is used in the standardization method:

$z = (x - u) / s$

Where z represents the new value, x represents the old value, u represents the mean, and s represents the standard deviation.

The first value as in the weight column from a data set above is 790, and a scaled value is:

$$(790 - 1292.23) / 238.74 = -2.1$$

The initial value in a volume column from all data set above is 1.0, so the scaled value is:

$$(1.0 - 1.61) / 0.38 = -1.59$$

Rather than comparing 790 to 1.0, you may instead compare -2.1 to -1.59.

A Python sklearn module contains a function called StandardScaler() that produces a Scaler object containing methods for altering data sets, so you don't have to do it manually.

Example:

All values throughout the Volume and Weight columns should be scaled as follows:

```
import pandas
from sklearn import linear_model
from sklearn.preprocessing import StandardScaler
scale = StandardScaler()

df = pandas.read_csv("cars2.csv")

X = df[['Weight', 'Volume']]

scaledX = scale.fit_transform(X)

print(scaledX)
```

Result:

```
[[-2.10389253 -1.59336644]
 [-0.55407235 -1.07190106]
 [-1.52166278 -1.59336644]
 [-1.78973979 -1.85409913]
 [-0.63784641 -0.28970299]
 [-1.52166278 -1.59336644]
 [-0.76769621 -0.55043568]
 [ 0.3046118  -0.28970299]
 [-0.7551301  -0.28970299]
 [-0.59595938 -0.0289703 ]
 [-1.30803892 -1.33263375]
 [-1.26615189 -0.81116837]
 [-0.7551301  -1.59336644]
 [-0.16871166 -0.0289703 ]
 [ 0.14125238 -0.0289703 ]
 [ 0.15800719 -0.0289703 ]
 [ 0.3046118  -0.0289703 ]
 [-0.05142797  1.53542584]
 [-0.72580918 -0.0289703 ]
 [ 0.14962979  1.01396046]
 [ 1.2219378  -0.0289703 ]
 [ 0.5685001   1.01396046]
 [ 0.3046118   1.27469315]
 [ 0.51404696 -0.0289703 ]
 [ 0.51404696  1.01396046]
 [ 0.72348212 -0.28970299]
 [ 0.8281997   1.01396046]
 [ 1.81254495  1.01396046]
 [ 0.96642691 -0.0289703 ]
 [ 1.72877089  1.01396046]
 [ 1.30990057  1.27469315]
 [ 1.90050772  1.01396046]
 [-0.23991961 -0.0289703 ]
 [ 0.40932938 -0.0289703 ]
 [ 0.47215993 -0.0289703 ]
 [ 0.4302729   2.31762392]]
```

Predict CO2 Values

As in the Multiple Regression chapter, you had to forecast how much CO2 an automobile will emit based on its weight and volume.

You must utilize the scale when predicting values if a data set is scaled:

Example:

Calculate the CO2 emissions from a 2300 kilogram 1.3 liter car:

```python
import pandas
from sklearn import linear_model
from sklearn.preprocessing import StandardScaler
scale = StandardScaler()

df = pandas.read_csv("cars2.csv")

X = df[['Weight', 'Volume']]
y = df['CO2']

scaledX = scale.fit_transform(X)

regr = linear_model.LinearRegression()
regr.fit(scaledX, y)

scaled = scale.transform([[2300, 1.3]])

predictedCO2 = regr.predict([scaled[0]])
print(predictedCO2)
```

Result:

```
[107.2087328]
```

3.13 Train/ Test

Assess Your Model

In Machine Learning, we develop models to predict the result of certain events, such as the CO2 emissions of a vehicle based on its weight and engine size in the previous chapter.

We may use the Train/Test technique to see if a model is effective enough.

What is Train/Test?

Train/Test is a technique for determining your model's correctness.

Because you divide that data set across two sets named as a training set or a testing set, it's termed Train/Test.

Training accounts for 80% of the budget while testing accounts for 20%.

The training set is used to train the model.

The testing set is used to test the model.

The term "train the model" refers to the process of developing a model.

Testing the model entails determining its correctness.

Start With a Data Set

Begin by selecting a data set to test.

Our data set depicts the purchasing behavior of 100 clients at a store.

Example:

```
import numpy
import matplotlib.pyplot as plt
numpy.random.seed(2)

x = numpy.random.normal(3, 1, 100)
y = numpy.random.normal(150, 40, 100) / x

plt.scatter(x, y)
plt.show()
```

Result:

The duration of minutes before making a transaction is shown on the x-axis.

The amount paid on the purchase is shown on the y axis.

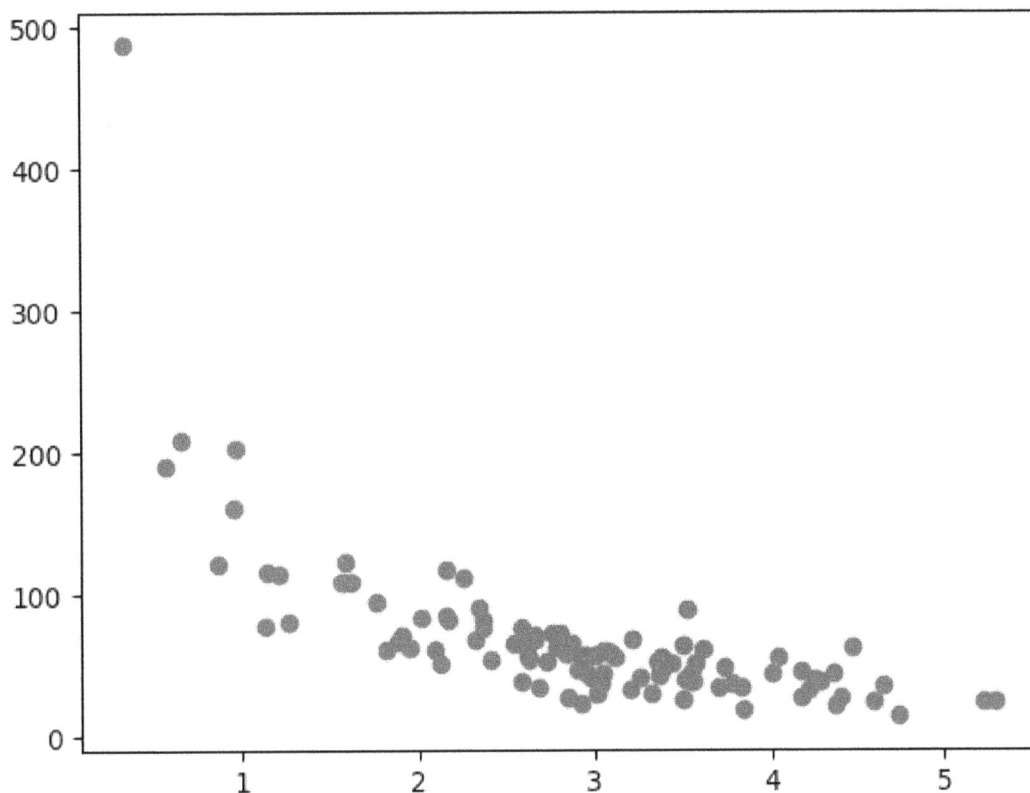

Split Into Train/Test

The random selection of over 80 percent of its total original data should be used as the training set.

The remaining 20% should be used for testing.

```
train_x = x[:80]
train_y = y[:80]

test_x = x[80:]
test_y = y[80:]
```

Display the Training Set

Display the training set's scatter plot as well:

Example:

```
plt.scatter(train_x, train_y)
plt.show()
```

Result:

It seems to be a good pick, as it appears to be the original data set:

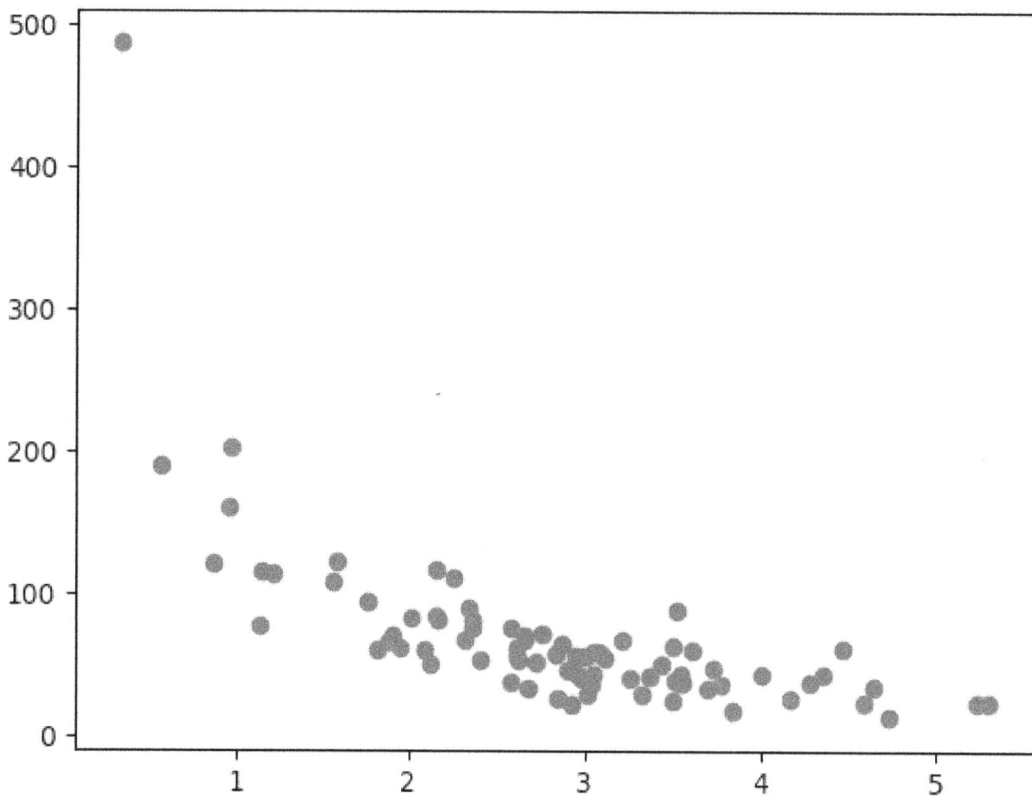

Display the Testing Set

We'll also look just at the testing set to make sure it's not radically different.

Example:

```
plt.scatter(test_x, test_y)
plt.show()
```

Result:

The testing set resembles an original data set in appearance:

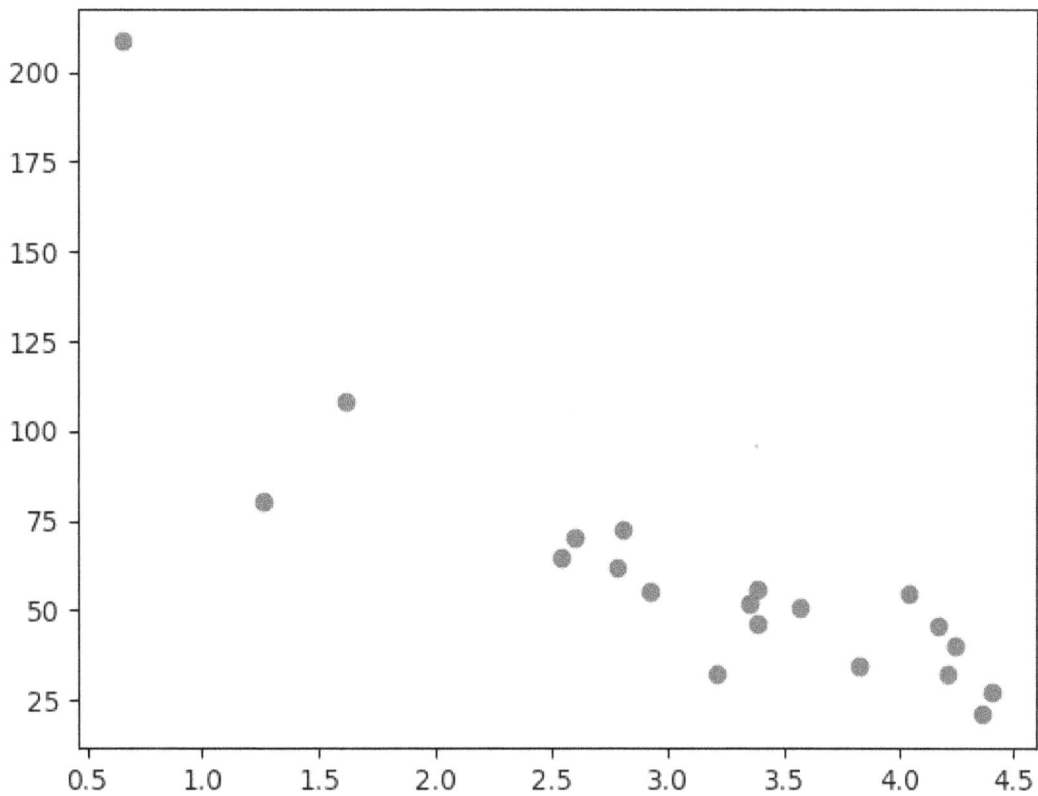

Fit the Data Set

How will the data set appear? A polynomial regression, in my view, would be the best match, therefore let's create a polynomial regression line.

The plot() function of a matplotlib module is used to create a line across the data points:

Example:

Connect the data points using a polynomial regression line:

```python
import numpy
import matplotlib.pyplot as plt
numpy.random.seed(2)

x = numpy.random.normal(3, 1, 100)
y = numpy.random.normal(150, 40, 100) / x

train_x = x[:80]
train_y = y[:80]

test_x = x[80:]
test_y = y[80:]

mymodel = numpy.poly1d(numpy.polyfit(train_x, train_y, 4))

myline = numpy.linspace(0, 6, 100)

plt.scatter(train_x, train_y)
plt.plot(myline, mymodel(myline))
plt.show()
```

Result:

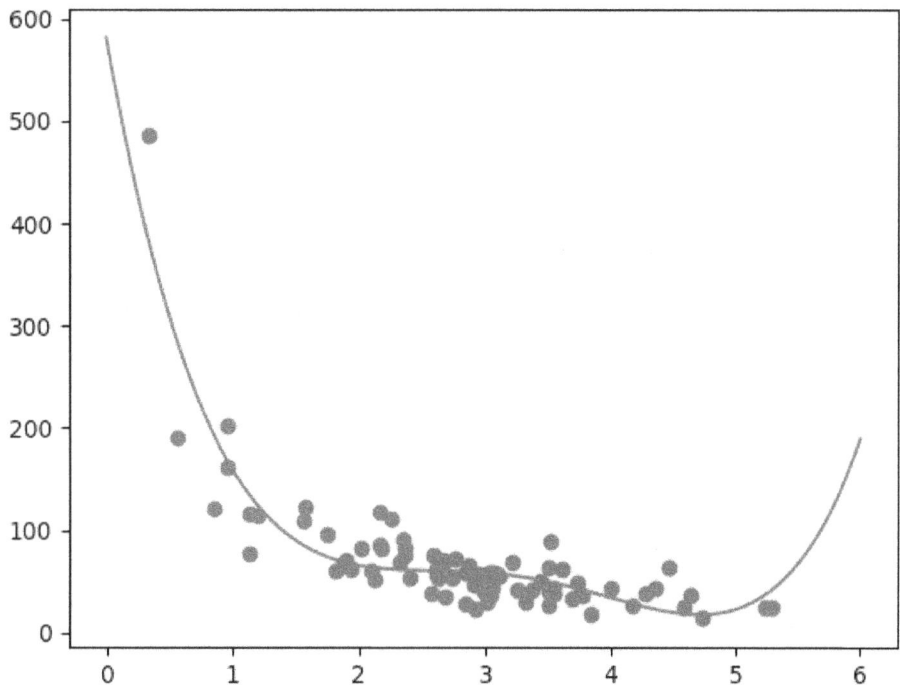

Even while it might give us some strange results if we tried to forecast values beyond the data set, the outcome supports my recommendation of fitting the data set to a polynomial regression. For example, the line suggests that a consumer who spends 6 minutes inside the store will spend $200. Overfitting is most likely the cause of this.

R2

R2, often known as R-squared, comes to mind?

It quantifies the connection between the x and y axes, with a value ranging from 0 to 1, with 0 indicating no connection and 1 indicating a complete connection.

The r2 score() function in the sklearn module will assist us in determining this connection.

In this situation, we'd want to see whether there's a link between the number of minutes a customer spends in the store and the amount of money they spend.

Example:

In a polynomial regression, how well would my training data fit?

The result of 0.799 indicates that the relationship is satisfactory ok.

```python
import numpy
from sklearn.metrics import r2_score
numpy.random.seed(2)

x = numpy.random.normal(3, 1, 100)
y = numpy.random.normal(150, 40, 100) / x

train_x = x[:80]
train_y = y[:80]

test_x = x[80:]
test_y = y[80:]

mymodel = numpy.poly1d(numpy.polyfit(train_x, train_y, 4))

r2 = r2_score(train_y, mymodel(train_x))

print(r2)
```

Bring in the Testing Set

Now we have the acceptable model, at least in terms of training data.

We want to verify the model using the testing data to check whether it produces the same results.

Example:

Let's see how to calculate the R2 score while utilizing testing data:

```
import numpy
from sklearn.metrics import r2_score
numpy.random.seed(2)

x = numpy.random.normal(3, 1, 100)
y = numpy.random.normal(150, 40, 100) / x

train_x = x[:80]
train_y = y[:80]

test_x = x[80:]
test_y = y[80:]

mymodel = numpy.poly1d(numpy.polyfit(train_x, train_y, 4))

r2 = r2_score(test_y, mymodel(test_x))

print(r2)
```

The result of 0.809 indicates that the model also matches the testing set, and we are sure that we can use it to forecast future values.

Predict Values

We can start forecasting new values now that we've demonstrated that this model is valid.

Example:

How much will a shopping consumer spend if he or she spends 5 minutes in the store?

```
print(mymodel(5))
```

Output:

The example predicted the customer to spend 22.88 dollars, as seems to correspond to the diagram:

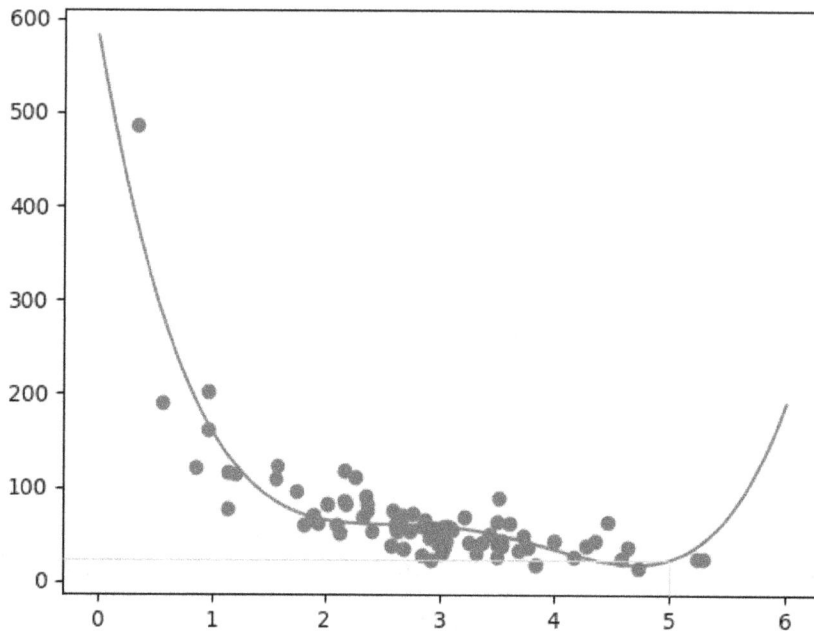

3.14 Decision Tree

The Decision Tree is a type of flow chart that may assist you in making choices based on past experience.

In an example, an individual is trying to determine whether or not to attend a comedy concert.

Fortunately, our example individual has registered each time a comedy event was scheduled in town, as well as some information on the comic and whether or not he or she attended.

Python can now design a decision tree based upon the data set to determine whether any new releases are worth seeing.

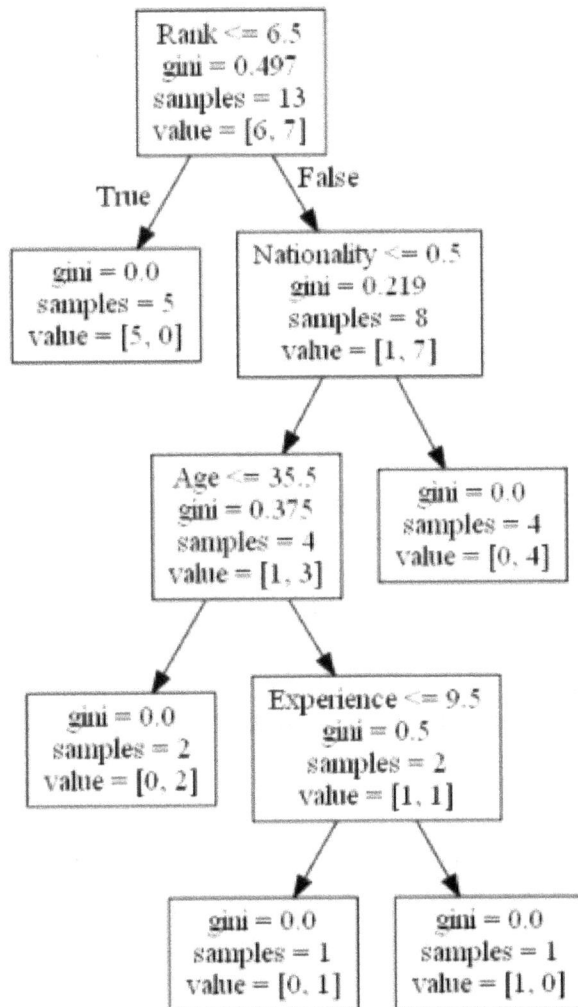

Working of decision tree:

First, load the modules you'll need, and then use pandas to read the dataset:

Example:

Read the data set and print it:

```
import pandas
from sklearn import tree
import pydotplus
from sklearn.tree import DecisionTreeClassifier
import matplotlib.pyplot as plt
import matplotlib.image as pltimg

df = pandas.read_csv("shows.csv")

print(df)
```

To create a decision tree, each of the information must be numerical.

The non-numerical columns 'Go' and 'Nationality' must be converted to numerical values.

The map() function in Pandas accepts a dictionary containing instructions on how to transform the values.

'UK': 0, 'USA': 1, 'N': 2' shows that convert 'UK' to 0, 'USA' to 1 then 'N' to 2.

Example:

Then we must segregate all feature columns from their target column by converting string values to numerical values.

```
d = {'UK': 0, 'USA': 1, 'N': 2}
df['Nationality'] = df['Nationality'].map(d)
d = {'YES': 1, 'NO': 0}
df['Go'] = df['Go'].map(d)

print(df)
```

These feature columns are just the ones we're trying to predict from, whereas the target column contains the values we're trying to forecast.

Example:

The feature columns are X, and the target column is y:

```
features = ['Age', 'Experience', 'Rank', 'Nationality']

X = df[features]
y = df['Go']

print(X)
print(y)
```

Now we can make the decision tree itself, fill it up with our information, and save it as an a.png file upon this computer:

Example:

Make the Decision Tree, saving it as a picture, and display it as follows:

```
dtree = DecisionTreeClassifier()
dtree = dtree.fit(X, y)
data = tree.export_graphviz(dtree, out_file=None, feature_names=features)
graph = pydotplus.graph_from_dot_data(data)
graph.write_png('mydecisiontree.png')

img=pltimg.imread('mydecisiontree.png')
imgplot = plt.imshow(img)
plt.show()
```

Python Feature Selection for Machine Learning

Feature selection is actually a method of selecting the characteristics in the data that give most to an output or prediction variable that you're interested in.

Many models, notably linear methods such as logistic or linear regression, suffer from the presence of irrelevant characteristics in their data.

The following are three advantages of completing selection of feature right before modeling your data:

Reduces Overfitting: When there is less duplicated data, there is less chance of making conclusions predicted on noise.

Modeling accuracy increases as a result of less/no deceptive data.

Lessens Training Time: With less data, algorithms may learn more quickly.

Machine Learning Feature Selection

Further section offers methods for feature selection techniques in Python.

Every recipe was created to be comprehensive and self-contained, allowing you to copy-and-paste it into your project and utilize it right away.

To explain the feature selection process, Recipes utilizes a Pima Indian diabetes dataset onset. It is the binary segmentation issue with just number attributes.

- Dataset Details.

- Dataset File.

1. Univariate Selection

Statistical tests may be performed to identify which attributes have the strongest link to an output variable.

The SelectKBest class in the scikit-learn package may be used with a variety of statistical tests to choose a certain range of attributes.

By this selection procedure, a variety of statistical tests may be applied. The ANOVA F-value approach, for example, is suited for categorical and numerical data, as shown in a Pima dataset. The f classif() method may be used to do this. In the example below, we'll use this strategy to choose the top four characteristics.

```
1  # Feature Selection with Univariate Statistical Tests
2  from pandas import read_csv
3  from numpy import set_printoptions
4  from sklearn.feature_selection import SelectKBest
5  from sklearn.feature_selection import f_classif
6  # load data
7  filename = 'pima-indians-diabetes.data.csv'
8  names = ['preg', 'plas', 'pres', 'skin', 'test', 'mass', 'pedi', 'age', 'class']
9  dataframe = read_csv(filename, names=names)
10 array = dataframe.values
11 X = array[:,0:8]
12 Y = array[:,8]
13 # feature extraction
14 test = SelectKBest(score_func=f_classif, k=4)
15 fit = test.fit(X, Y)
16 # summarize scores
17 set_printoptions(precision=3)
18 print(fit.scores_)
19 features = fit.transform(X)
20 # summarize selected features
21 print(features[0:5,:])
```

Because of the nonlinear dynamics of an algorithm or assessment technique, as well as changes in numerical accuracy, your findings may vary. Consider repeating the procedure and comparing the average result.

```
1  [ 39.67  213.162   3.257   4.304  13.281  71.772  23.871  46.141]
2
3  [[   6.   148.    33.6  50. ]
4   [   1.    85.    26.6  31. ]
5   [   8.   183.    23.3  32. ]
6   [   1.    89.    28.1  21. ]
7   [   0.   137.    43.1  33. ]]
```

You can see the scores for each attribute and the 4 attributes chosen.

2. Recursive Feature Elimination

Recursive Feature Elimination or RFE works by deleting characteristics iteratively and creating a model on the remaining attributes.

It determines which qualities (and combinations of characteristics) offer the most to determining the desired characteristic using model accuracy.

```
1  # Feature Extraction with RFE
2  from pandas import read_csv
3  from sklearn.feature_selection import RFE
4  from sklearn.linear_model import LogisticRegression
5  # load data
6  url = "https://raw.githubusercontent.com/jbrownlee/Datasets/master/pima-indians-di
7  names = ['preg', 'plas', 'pres', 'skin', 'test', 'mass', 'pedi', 'age', 'class']
8  dataframe = read_csv(url, names=names)
9  array = dataframe.values
10 X = array[:,0:8]
11 Y = array[:,8]
12 # feature extraction
13 model = LogisticRegression(solver='lbfgs')
14 rfe = RFE(model, 3)
15 fit = rfe.fit(X, Y)
16 print("Num Features: %d" % fit.n_features_)
17 print("Selected Features: %s" % fit.support_)
18 print("Feature Ranking: %s" % fit.ranking_)
```

To choose the top three characteristics, the example following uses RFE in conjunction with a logistic regression methodology. It doesn't matter whatever algorithm you choose as long as it's smart and consistent.

```
1  Num Features: 3
2  Selected Features: [ True False False False False  True  True False]
3  Feature Ranking: [1 2 3 5 6 1 1 4]
```

As you can see, RFE picked preg, mass, and pedi as the top three attributes.

These are denoted with the chosen one in the ranking_ array and True in a support array.

Principal Component Analysis

Principal Component Analysis or PCA compresses a dataset by applying linear algebra to it.

This is often referred to as a data reduction approach. PCA has the advantage of allowing you to select many dimensions and primary components in the converted outcome.

```
1  # Feature Extraction with PCA
2  import numpy
3  from pandas import read_csv
4  from sklearn.decomposition import PCA
5  # load data
6  url = "https://raw.githubusercontent.com/jbrownlee/Datasets/master/pima-indians-di
7  names = ['preg', 'plas', 'pres', 'skin', 'test', 'mass', 'pedi', 'age', 'class']
8  dataframe = read_csv(url, names=names)
9  array = dataframe.values
10 X = array[:,0:8]
11 Y = array[:,8]
12 # feature extraction
13 pca = PCA(n_components=3)
14 fit = pca.fit(X)
15 # summarize components
16 print("Explained Variance: %s" % fit.explained_variance_ratio_)
17 print(fit.components_)
```

We'll use PCA to determine three main components in the sample below.

```
1  Explained Variance: [ 0.88854663  0.06159078  0.02579012]
2  [[ -2.02176587e-03   9.78115765e-02   1.60930503e-02   6.07566861e-02
3     9.93110844e-01   1.40108085e-02   5.37167919e-04  -3.56474430e-03]
4   [  2.26488861e-02   9.72210040e-01   1.41909330e-01  -5.78614699e-02
5     -9.46266913e-02   4.69729766e-02   8.16804621e-04   1.40168181e-01]
6   [ -2.24649003e-02   1.43428710e-01  -9.22467192e-01  -3.07013055e-01
7     2.09773019e-02  -1.32444542e-01  -6.39983017e-04  -1.25454310e-01]]
```

The modified dataset (3 main components) has little similarity to the raw data, as can be shown.

Feature Importance

To evaluate the value of characteristics, bagged decision trees such as Extra Trees and Random Forest may be employed.

For such Pima Indian onset of diabetes dataset, we build an ExtraTreesClassifier classifier in the example below. The scikit-learn API has further information about the ExtraTreesClassifier class.

```
1  # Feature Importance with Extra Trees Classifier
2  from pandas import read_csv
3  from sklearn.ensemble import ExtraTreesClassifier
4  # load data
5  url = "https://raw.githubusercontent.com/jbrownlee/Datasets/master/pima-indians-d
6  names = ['preg', 'plas', 'pres', 'skin', 'test', 'mass', 'pedi', 'age', 'class']
7  dataframe = read_csv(url, names=names)
8  array = dataframe.values
9  X = array[:,0:8]
10 Y = array[:,8]
11 # feature extraction
12 model = ExtraTreesClassifier(n_estimators=10)
13 model.fit(X, Y)
14 print(model.feature_importances_)
```

As you can see, each attribute is assigned a significance score, with the higher the value, the more significant the attribute. The results point to the significance of plas, age, and mass.

```
1  [ 0.11070069  0.2213717   0.08824115  0.08068703  0.07281761  0.14548537 0.12654214
```

Chapter 4: Basic Syntax of the Python

Python has a lot of similarities with C, Perl, and Java. There are, nevertheless, some clear distinctions between the languages. A parser reads a Python program. Python was created to be a very readable programming language. The Python programming language's syntax is a collection of rules that dictate how a Python program is constructed.

4.1 Basic Python Program

Let's run several programs in various programming styles.

Interactive Mode Programming

When you use the interpreter without specifying a script file as an argument, you'll get the following message:

```
$ python
Python 2.4.3 (#1, Nov 11 2010, 13:34:43)
[GCC 4.1.2 20080704 (Red Hat 4.1.2-48)] on linux2
Type "help", "copyright", "credits" or "license" for more information.
>>>
```

At the Python prompt, write the following text and hit Enter.

```
>>> print "Hello, Python!"
```

If you're using a newer version of Python, you'll need to use the print statement with parentheses, as seen below. Hello, Python! In Python 2.4.3, however, this yields the following result.

```
Hello, Python!
```

Script Mode Programming

Invoking an interpreter with the script argument starts the script's execution and continues until it is completed. The interpreter is turned off after the script is done.

Let's develop a script for a basic Python app. The extension.py is used for Python files. In a test.py file, write the below source code:

```
print "Hello, Python!"
```

We'll presume you've placed the Python interpreter in your PATH variable. Now, try running this program like this:

```
$ python test.py
```

As a consequence of this, the following result is obtained:

```
Hello, Python!
```

Let's have a look at another technique to run a Python script. The amended test.py file may be found here:

```
#!/usr/bin/python

print "Hello, Python!"
```

We'll assume you have the Python interpreter in your /usr/bin directory. Now, try running this program like this:

```
$ chmod +x test.py      # This is to make file executable
$ ./test.py
```

As a consequence of this, the following result is obtained:

```
Hello, Python!
```

4.2 Python Identifiers

The Python identifier is really a name for a function, variable, class, module, or another object in Python. An identifier begins with a letter from A to Z, or a to z, or an underscore (_), then zero or even more letters, underscores, or numbers (0 to 9).

Within identifiers, punctuation characters like @, $, and percent are not allowed. Python is a programming language that is case-sensitive. As a result, in Python, manpower & Manpower are two separate identifiers.

The naming standards for Python identifiers are as follows:

- The name of the class begins using an uppercase letter. The beginning of all other identifiers is a lowercase letter.

- The presence of a single lead underscore in an identifier implies that it is private.

- An identification that begins with two lead underscores is considered to be very secret.

- An identifier is a language defined special name if it also terminates with two trailing underscores.

4.3 Reserved Words

The Python keywords are shown in the table below. You can't use these terms as constants, variables, and any similar identifier name since they're reserved. Only lowercase characters appear in the Python keywords.

and	exec	not
assert	finally	or
break	for	pass
class	from	print
continue	global	raise
def	if	return
del	import	try
elif	in	while
else	is	with
except	lambda	yield

4.4 Lines and Indentation

There are no brackets in Python to mark code blocks for function and class declarations or flow control. Line indentation, which is strictly enforced, is used to designate code blocks.

The indentation may be any number of spaces, but all statements as in block should be indented the same amount. For instance:

```
if True:
    print "True"
else:
    print "False"
```

The next block, however, produces an error:

```
if True:
print "Answer"
print "True"
else:
print "Answer"
print "False"
```

Thus, in Python, a block is formed by all continuous lines indented by the same amount of spaces. Various statement blocks are used in the following example:

```python
#!/usr/bin/python

import sys

try:
    # open file stream
    file = open(file_name, "w")
except IOError:
    print "There was an error writing to", file_name
    sys.exit()
print "Enter '", file_finish,
print "' When finished"
while file_text != file_finish:
    file_text = raw_input("Enter text: ")
    if file_text == file_finish:
        # close the file
        file.close
        break
    file.write(file_text)
    file.write("\n")
file.close()
file_name = raw_input("Enter filename: ")
if len(file_name) == 0:
    print "Next time please enter something"
    sys.exit()
try:
    file = open(file_name, "r")
except IOError:
    print "There was an error reading file"
    sys.exit()
file_text = file.read()
file.close()
print file_text
```

4.5 Multi-Line Statements

In Python, statements usually conclude on a new line. A line continuation character () in Python, on the other hand, may be used to indicate that a line should continue. Such as:

```python
total = item_one + \
        item_two + \
        item_three
```

A line continuation character is not required for statements enclosed in the [],() or {}. For example in the case:

```
days = ['Monday', 'Tuesday', 'Wednesday',
        'Thursday', 'Friday']
```

4.6 Quotation in Python

To designate string literals, Python allows single ('), double ("), and triple ("' or """) quotes, as long as the same kind of quotation begins and ends the string.

To spread the string over many lines, triple quotes are utilized. All of the following, for example, is lawful:

```
word = 'word'
sentence = "This is a sentence."
paragraph = """This is a paragraph. It is
made up of multiple lines and sentences."""
```

4.7 Comments in Python

A comment starts with a hash mark (#) outside of a string literal. A Python interpreter ignores any characters following the # and up till the end of a physical line as part of the remark.

```
#!/usr/bin/python

# First comment
print "Hello, Python!" # second comment
```

As a consequence of this, the following result is obtained:

```
Hello, Python!
```

Following a statement or expression, you may write a remark on the same line:

```
name = "Madisetti" # This is again comment
```

You may remark on many lines in the same way:

```
# This is a comment.
# This is a comment, too.
# This is a comment, too.
# I said that already.
```

The Python interpreter ignores the following triple-quoted text, which may be applied as a multiline comment:

```
'''
This is a multiline
comment.
'''
```

Using Blank Lines

A blank line is a line that has simply whitespace, potentially with a comment, and Python ignores it completely.

To end a multiline statement during an interactive interpreter process, type an empty physical line.

Waiting for the User

The program's next line shows the prompt and the phrase "Press your enter key to leave," and then waits for a user to respond:

Before showing the real line, "\n\n" is used to produce two additional lines. The application finishes when the user pushes the key. This is a clever way to keep a terminal window active until the user has completed their task.

Multiple Statements on a Single Line

If neither statement begins a new code block, a semicolon (;) permits several statements on a single line. Here's an example of how to use the semicolon:

```
import sys; x = 'foo'; sys.stdout.write(x + '\n')
```

Multiple Statement Groups as Suites

In Python, a suite is a collection of discrete statements that form a single code block. The header line or a suite are required for compound or complicated statements like while, if, def, and class.

The statement containing the keyword is started with a header line, which ends with a colon (:), and is continued by one or multiple lines that build up the suite.

For instance:

```
if expression :
    suite
elif expression :
    suite
else :
    suite
```

Command Line Arguments

Many applications may be launched to offer you basic instructions on how to use them. This is possible using Python's -h – helper function.

```
$ python -h
usage: python [option] ... [-c cmd | -m mod | file | -] [arg] ...
Options and arguments (and corresponding environment variables):
-c cmd : program passed in as string (terminates option list)
-d     : debug output from parser (also PYTHONDEBUG=x)
-E     : ignore environment variables (such as PYTHONPATH)
-h     : print this help message and exit

[ etc. ]
```

You may also program your script such that it accepts a variety of parameters.

4.8 Python Coding Style

There should be four spaces between each indentation with no tabs.

Do not use tabs and spaces in the same sentence. Tabs cause confusion, therefore it's best to stick to using just spaces.

Users with a tiny display will appreciate the maximum line length of 79 characters.

Split class and top-level function declarations with blank lines, and use a solitary blank line to differentiate methods declarations within a class and bigger chunks of code within functions.

Inline comments should be used whenever feasible should be complete sentences.

Around expressions and assertions, use spaces.

Python Reserve words:

The identifiers listed below are reserved terms in the language that can be used as regular identifiers.

False	class	finally	is	return
None	continue	for	lambda	try
True	def	from	nonlocal	while
and	del	global	not	with
as	el	if	or	yield
assert	else	import	pass	
break	except	in	raise	

Chapter 5: Statements in python

A Python Statement

Statements are the instructions that a Python interpreter may carry out. An assignment statement, for example, is a = 1. Other types of statements include if statements, for statements, while statements, and so on, which will be addressed later.

Multi-line statement

A newline character is used to indicate the conclusion of a statement in Python. However, using the line continuation character, we may have a statement span many lines (\). Consider the following scenario:

```
a = 1 + 2 + 3 + \
    4 + 5 + 6 + \
    7 + 8 + 9
```

This is a line continuation that is explicitly stated. Brackets [ ], Parentheses ( ), and braces { } in Python imply line continuation. For example, we may write the multi-line sentence as follows:

```
a = (1 + 2 + 3 +
    4 + 5 + 6 +
    7 + 8 + 9)
```

The line continuation is implied by the enclosing parenthesis ( ). The same is true for [ ] and. Consider the following scenario:

```
colors = ['red',
          'blue',
          'green']
```

We may also use semicolons to place numerous statements on a single line, as seen below:

```
a = 1; b = 2; c = 3
```

Chapter 6: Dictionaries in python

The dictionary in python is actually a list of elements that are not in any particular order. A dictionary contains a key/value pair for each entry.

When the key is known, dictionaries are optimized to retrieve values.

6.1 Creating Python Dictionary

It's as easy as putting things within curly braces and separating them with commas to make a dictionary.

The one item has one key and its value, which are stated as a pair key as a value.

Although values may be of either any data type and may be repeated, keys necessarily be unique and of an immutable type i.e. integer, string or tuple along immutable members.

```python
# empty dictionary
my_dict = {}

# dictionary with integer keys
my_dict = {1: 'apple', 2: 'ball'}

# dictionary with mixed keys
my_dict = {'name': 'John', 1: [2, 4, 3]}

# using dict()
my_dict = dict({1:'apple', 2:'ball'})

# from sequence having each item as a pair
my_dict = dict([(1,'apple'), (2,'ball')])
```

So you can observe from the above example, in addition we can use the built-in dict() method to construct a dictionary.

6.2 Accessing Elements from Dictionary

While other data types utilize indexing to obtain values, a dictionary employs keys. Keys may be utilized using the get() function or within square brackets [].

When we use square brackets [], we get a KeyError if a key isn't located in the dictionary. The get() function, but on the other hand, yields None if a key isn't found.

```
# get vs [] for retrieving elements
my_dict = {'name': 'Jack', 'age': 26}

# Output: Jack
print(my_dict['name'])

# Output: 26
print(my_dict.get('age'))

# Trying to access keys which doesn't exist throws error
# Output None
print(my_dict.get('address'))

# KeyError
print(my_dict['address'])
```

Output:

```
Jack
26
None
Traceback (most recent call last):
  File "<string>", line 15, in <module>
    print(my_dict['address'])
KeyError: 'address'
```

6.3 Changing and Adding Dictionary elements

Dictionaries are subject to change. Using the assignment operator, we may create latest items or alter the value of already presented ones.

If the key already exists, the existing value will be changed. If the key is missing, the dictionary is updated with a new key as a value pair.

```python
# Changing and adding Dictionary Elements
my_dict = {'name': 'Jack', 'age': 26}

# update value
my_dict['age'] = 27

#Output: {'age': 27, 'name': 'Jack'}
print(my_dict)

# add item
my_dict['address'] = 'Downtown'

# Output: {'address': 'Downtown', 'age': 27, 'name': 'Jack'}
print(my_dict)
```

Output:

```
{'name': 'Jack', 'age': 27}
{'name': 'Jack', 'age': 27, 'address': 'Downtown'}
```

6.4 Removing elements from Dictionary

Using the pop() function, we may delete a specific item from a dictionary. This function returns the value after removing an item with a supplied key. The popitem() function removes and returns any key, value item pair from a dictionary. The clear() function may be used to delete all of the objects at once.

A keyword del may also be used to delete specific entries or the whole vocabulary.

```python
# create a dictionary
squares = {1: 1, 2: 4, 3: 9, 4: 16, 5: 25}

# remove a particular item, returns its value
# Output: 16
print(squares.pop(4))

# Output: {1: 1, 2: 4, 3: 9, 5: 25}
print(squares)

# remove an arbitrary item, return (key,value)
# Output: (5, 25)
print(squares.popitem())

# Output: {1: 1, 2: 4, 3: 9}
print(squares)

# remove all items
squares.clear()

# Output: {}
print(squares)

# delete the dictionary itself
del squares

# Throws Error
print(squares)
```

Output:

```
16
{1: 1, 2: 4, 3: 9, 5: 25}
(5, 25)
{1: 1, 2: 4, 3: 9}
{}
Traceback (most recent call last):
  File "<string>", line 30, in <module>
    print(squares)
NameError: name 'squares' is not defined
```

6.5 Methods for Python Dictionary

The methods that may be used with the dictionary are listed underneath. While few of these have previously been mentioned in the previous paragraphs.

Method	Description
clear()	Removes all items from the dictionary.
copy()	Returns a shallow copy of the dictionary.
fromkeys(seq[, v])	Returns a new dictionary with keys from `seq` and value equal to `v` (defaults to `None`).
get(key[,d])	Returns the value of the `key`. If the `key` does not exist, returns `d` (defaults to `None`).
items()	Return a new object of the dictionary's items in (key, value) format.
keys()	Returns a new object of the dictionary's keys.
pop(key[,d])	Removes the item with the `key` and returns its value or `d` if `key` is not found. If `d` is not provided and the `key` is not found, it raises `KeyError`.
popitem()	Removes and returns an arbitrary item (**key, value**). Raises `KeyError` if the dictionary is empty.
setdefault(key[,d])	Returns the corresponding value if the `key` is in the dictionary. If not, inserts the `key` with a value of `d` and returns `d` (defaults to `None`).
update([other])	Updates the dictionary with the key/value pairs from `other`, overwriting existing keys.
values()	Returns a new object of the dictionary's values

Following are a few examples of how these strategies may be used.

```python
# Dictionary Methods
marks = {}.fromkeys(['Math', 'English', 'Science'], 0)

# Output: {'English': 0, 'Math': 0, 'Science': 0}
print(marks)

for item in marks.items():
    print(item)

# Output: ['English', 'Math', 'Science']
print(list(sorted(marks.keys())))
```

Output:

```python
# Dictionary Methods
marks = {}.fromkeys(['Math', 'English', 'Science'], 0)

# Output: {'English': 0, 'Math': 0, 'Science': 0}
print(marks)

for item in marks.items():
    print(item)

# Output: ['English', 'Math', 'Science']
print(list(sorted(marks.keys())))
```

6.6 Python Dictionary Comprehension

In Python, dictionary comprehension is actually a simple and beautiful approach to generate a new dictionary via an iterable.

An expression pair key is a value follows by a for statement enclosed in curly braces in dictionary comprehension.

Here's an example of a dictionary for each entry consisting of a pair of numbers and their squares.

```
# Dictionary Comprehension
squares = {x: x*x for x in range(6)}

print(squares)
```

Output:

```
{0: 0, 1: 1, 2: 4, 3: 9, 4: 16, 5: 25}
```

This code is the same as

```
squares = {}
for x in range(6):
    squares[x] = x*x
print(squares)
```

Output:

```
{0: 0, 1: 1, 2: 4, 3: 9, 4: 16, 5: 25}
```

More for or if statements may be included in a dictionary comprehension if desired.

Items may be filtered out using the optional if statement to create a new dictionary.

Here are several examples of how to construct an odd-item dictionary.

```
# Dictionary Comprehension with if conditional
odd_squares = {x: x*x for x in range(11) if x % 2 == 1}

print(odd_squares)
```

Output:

```
{1: 1, 3: 9, 5: 25, 7: 49, 9: 81}
```

6.7 Other Dictionary Operations

Dictionary Membership Test

Using the term in, we can see whether the key will be in a dictionary or not. It's worth noting that a membership test only applies to the keys, not the values.

```python
# Membership Test for Dictionary Keys
squares = {1: 1, 3: 9, 5: 25, 7: 49, 9: 81}

# Output: True
print(1 in squares)

# Output: True
print(2 not in squares)

# membership tests for key only not value
# Output: False
print(49 in squares)
```

Output:

```
True
True
False
```

Using a Dictionary to Iterate

A for loop may be used to cycle across every key in the dictionary.

```
# Iterating through a Dictionary
squares = {1: 1, 3: 9, 5: 25, 7: 49, 9: 81}
for i in squares:
    print(squares[i])
```

Output:

```
1
9
25
49
81
```

Dictionary's Built-in Functions

All(), len(), cmp(), any(), sorted(), and other built-in methods are widely used along dictionaries to complete various tasks.

Function	Description
all()	Return True if all keys of the dictionary are True (or if the dictionary is empty).
any()	Return True if any key of the dictionary is true. If the dictionary is empty, return False.
len()	Return the length (the number of items) in the dictionary.
cmp()	Compares items of two dictionaries. (Not available in Python 3)
sorted()	Return a new sorted list of keys in the dictionary.

Below are some examples of how to operate with a dictionary using built-in functions.

```
# Dictionary Built-in Functions
squares = {0: 0, 1: 1, 3: 9, 5: 25, 7: 49, 9: 81}

# Output: False
print(all(squares))

# Output: True
print(any(squares))

# Output: 6
print(len(squares))

# Output: [0, 1, 3, 5, 7, 9]
print(sorted(squares))
```

Output:

```
False
True
6
[0, 1, 3, 5, 7, 9]
```

Chapter 7: First Project Of Python

Implementing the First Program

Step: 1

 Launch PyCharm Editor. The PyCharm introduction screen may be seen here. Click "Create New Project" to start a new project.

Step: 2

You'll have to choose a place.

You have the option of choosing the place where the project will be developed. Keep it as is if you don't want to alter the location, but change the title from "untitled" to something more significant, such as "FirstProject."

PyCharm should have discovered any Python interpreter you previously installed.

Then press the "Create" button.

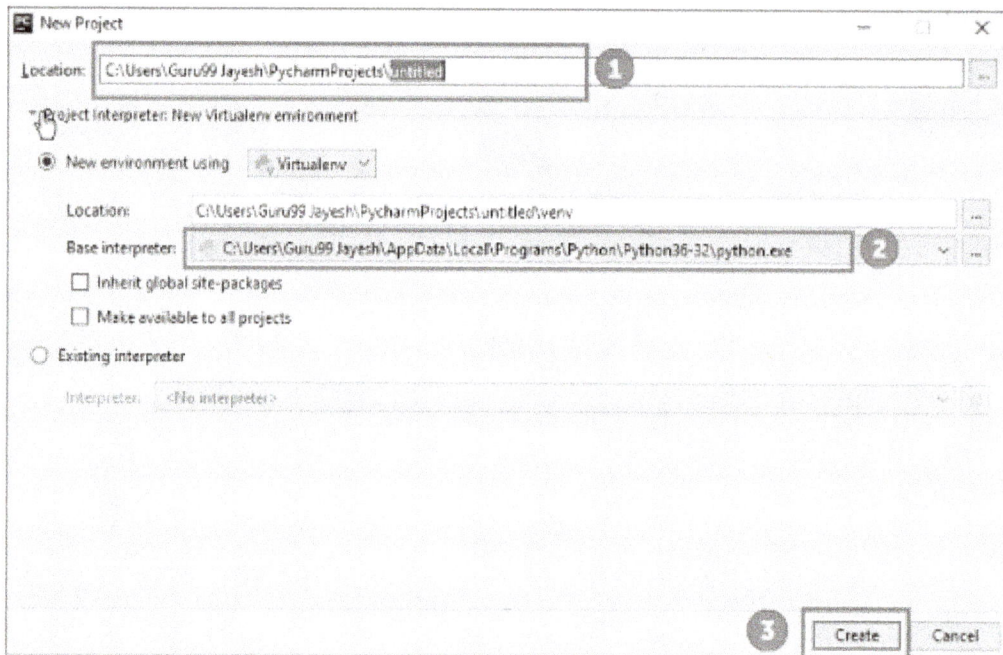

Step: 3

Now it's your turn. Go to the "File" menu and choose "New." After that, choose "Python File."

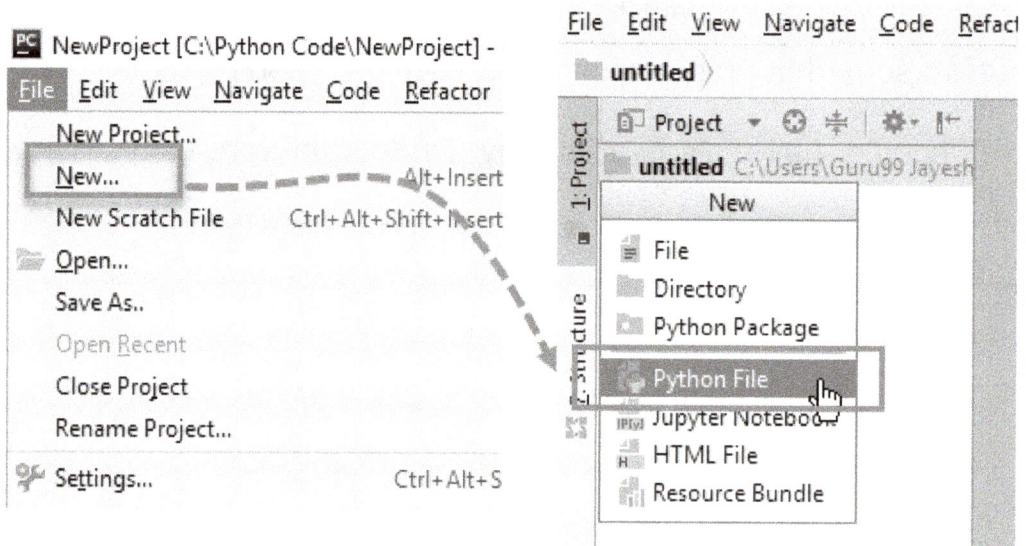

Step: 4

A new pop-up window will open. Now input the file's name (in this case, "HelloWorld") and click "OK."

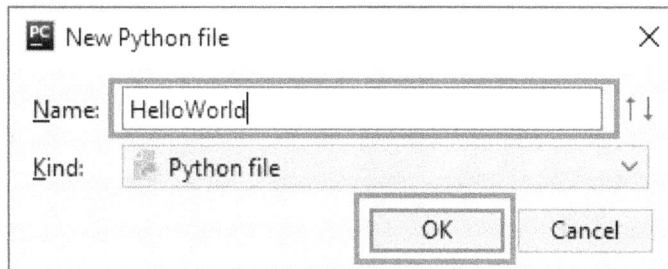

Step: 5

Now create a simple program called print ('Hello World!').

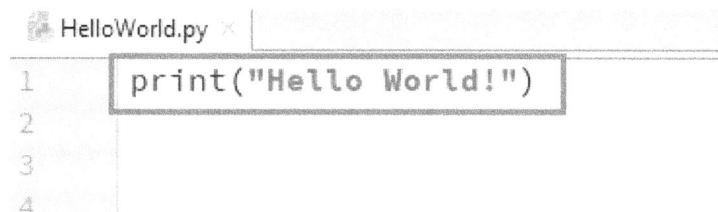

Step: 6

Now it's your turn. To execute your program, go to the "Run" menu and pick "Run."

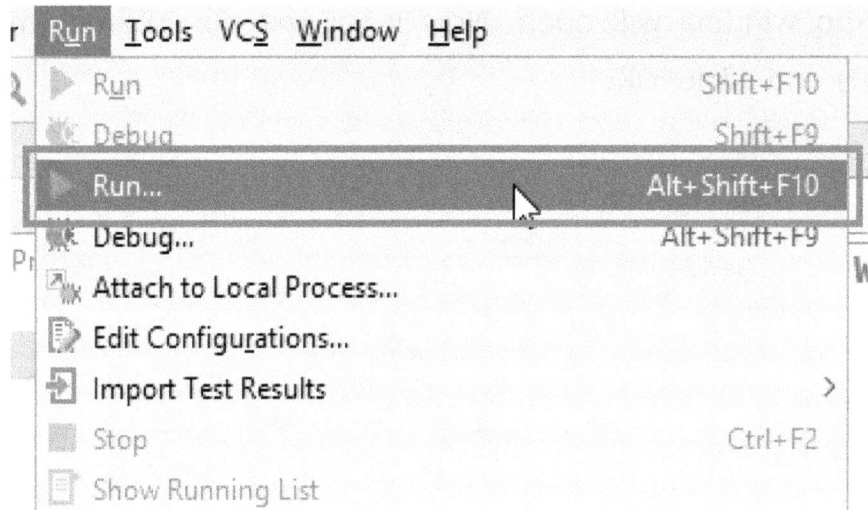

Step: 7

The result of your application may be shown at a bottom of the screen.

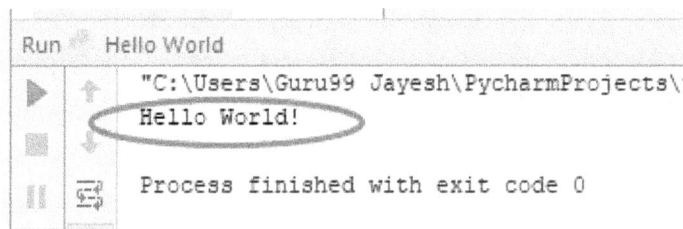

Step: 8

You may still execute a code from a command prompt if you're not using Pycharm Editor installed. To execute the software, type the right file location at the command prompt.

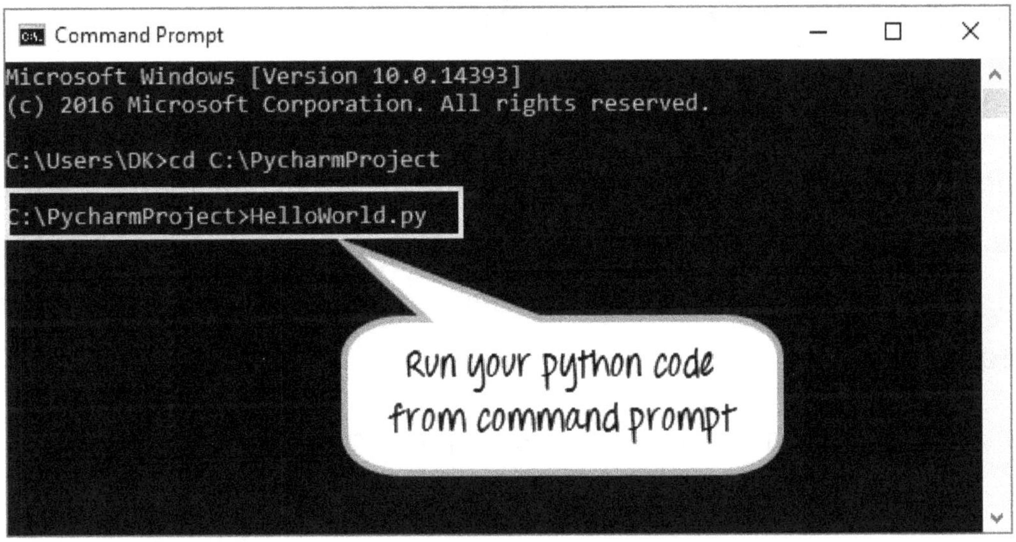

The code's output would be as follows:

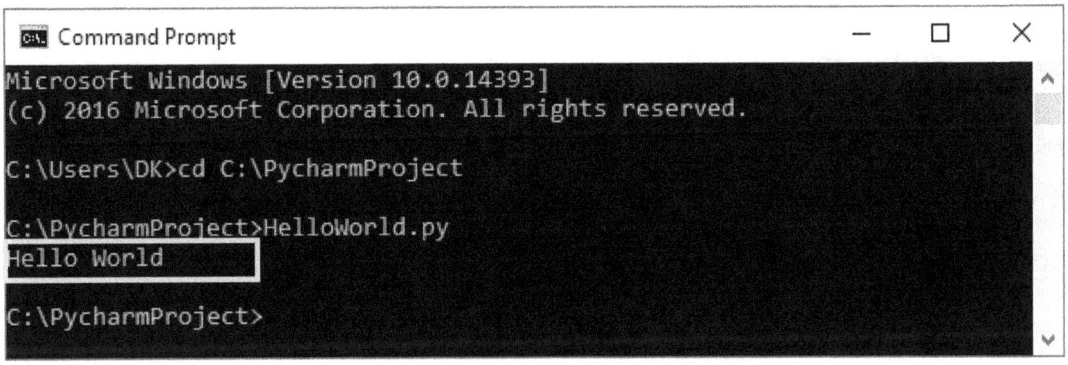

Chapter 8: Indexes In python

In Python, what is indexing?

In Python, indexing is a method of referring to particular elements inside an iterable based on their location. In other words, you may directly access your desired pieces inside an iterable and perform a variety of actions based on your requirements.

Before we go into Python indexing examples, there's something to keep in mind:

Objects in Python are "zero-indexed," which means the position count begins at zero. A similar pattern may be seen in many different programming languages. Because of its online popularity in meme culture, several of you should already be acquainted with it.

So, let's say there are five items on a list. The "zeroth" position is then held by an element i.e. the leftmost element, followed by the elements in a first, second, third, and fourth place.

```python
fruits = ["apple", "grape", "orange", "guava", "banana"]

#Printing out the indexes of Apples and Banana
print("Indedx of Apple: " + fruits.index("apple"))
print("Indedx of Banana: " + fruits.index("banana"))
```

Output:

```
Indedx of Apple: 0
Indedx of Banana: 4
```

Once an index() method is invoked on a list with an item name as a parameter, the index of a particular item inside the list may be exposed.

Finally, we'll look at how to utilize the index() function on iterable objects in the next section.

8.1 What is the Index Operator in Python?

A Python Index Operator is symbolized by square brackets that open and close: []. The syntax, on the other hand, necessitates the use of a number within the brackets.

Syntax of Python Index Operator:

```
ObjectName[n] #Where n is just an integer number that represents the position
```

8.2 Indexing in Python: A Step-by-Step Guide

We'll look at several instances of indexing in Python in the sections below.

1. Indexing Strings Output:

```
greetings = "Hello, World!"

print(greetings[0]) #Prints the 0-th element in our string

print(greetings[5]) #Prints the 5-th element in our string

print(greetins[12]) #Prints the 12-th element in our string
```

We can observe how our print method accesses several components inside our given string object to obtain the desired characters.

H
,
!

2. Negative Indexing in Python

We just learned how to utilize indexing in Strings and Lists to retrieve the precise objects we're looking for. Although we've used a positive integer within our index operator the square brackets in all of our prior examples, this isn't required.

Negative integers are often used if we are concerned about the final few members of a list or simply wish to index a list from the other end. Negative indexing is the technique of indexing from an opposite end.

```python
letters = ['a', 's', 'd', 'f']

#We want to print the last element of the list
print(letters[-1]) #Notice we didn't use -0

#To print the 2nd last element from an iterable
print(letters[-2])
```

The final element in negative indexing is denoted by -1 rather than -0.

Output:

f
d

Chapter 9: Installation of python

Python Installation Instructions; Set-up for Environment:

The first step toward becoming a Python developer is to understand how to install and update Python on any local system or computer. We'll go through how to install Python on different operating systems in this article.

9.1 Installation on Windows:

To get the newest version of Python, go to https://www.python.org/downloads/. We will install Python 3.8.6 on the Windows operating system through this procedure. When we click the link above, we will be sent to the following website.

1st step:

Choose the Python version you want to download.

Select the "Download" option from the drop-down menu.

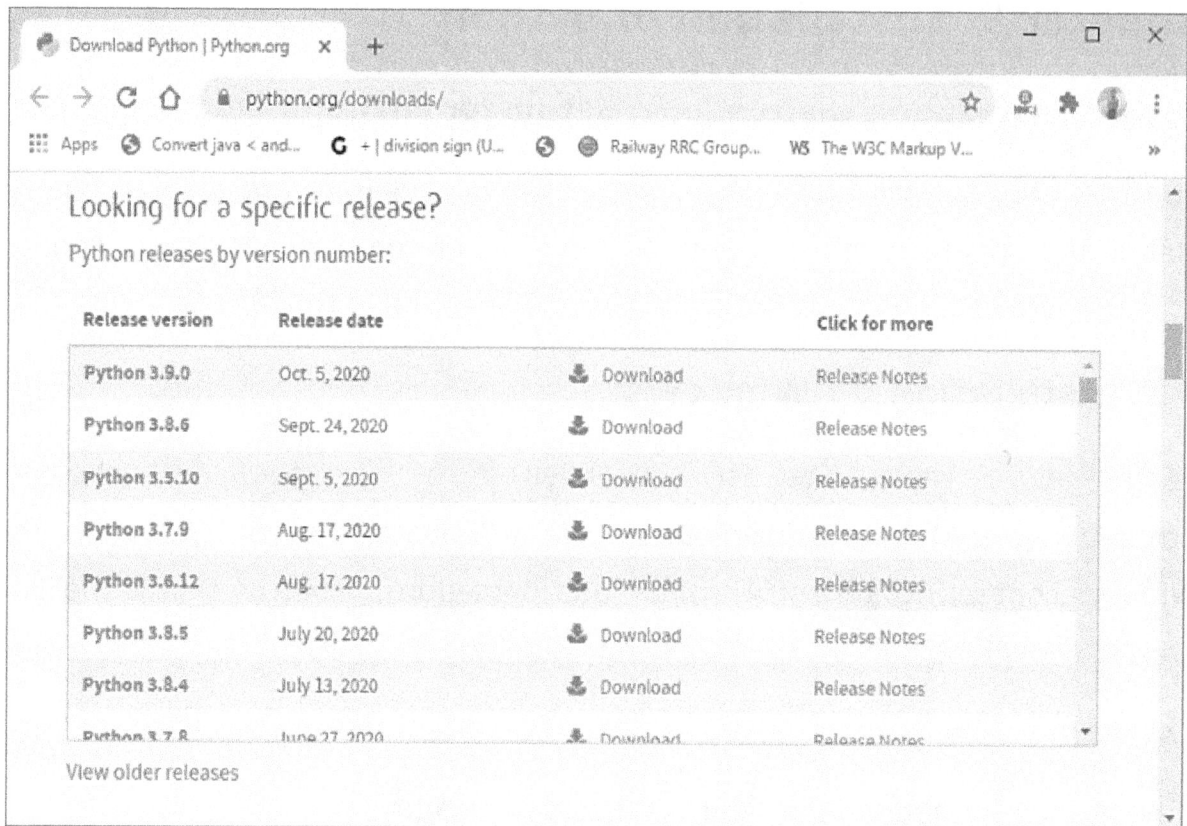

Step 2:

Select the Install Now option.

Double-click the downloaded executable file to bring up the following window. Proceed by selecting Customize installation. When you choose to Add a Path check box, the Python path will be automatically configured.

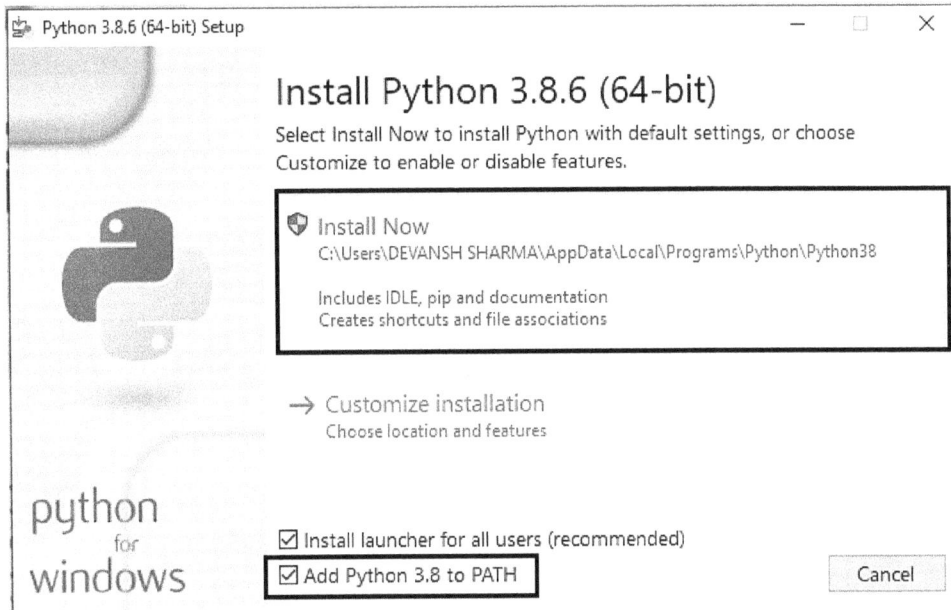

We may also choose the required location and features by clicking on the customize installation button. Another key factor to consider is whether or not to install a launcher for all users.

Step 3:

In-Process Installation

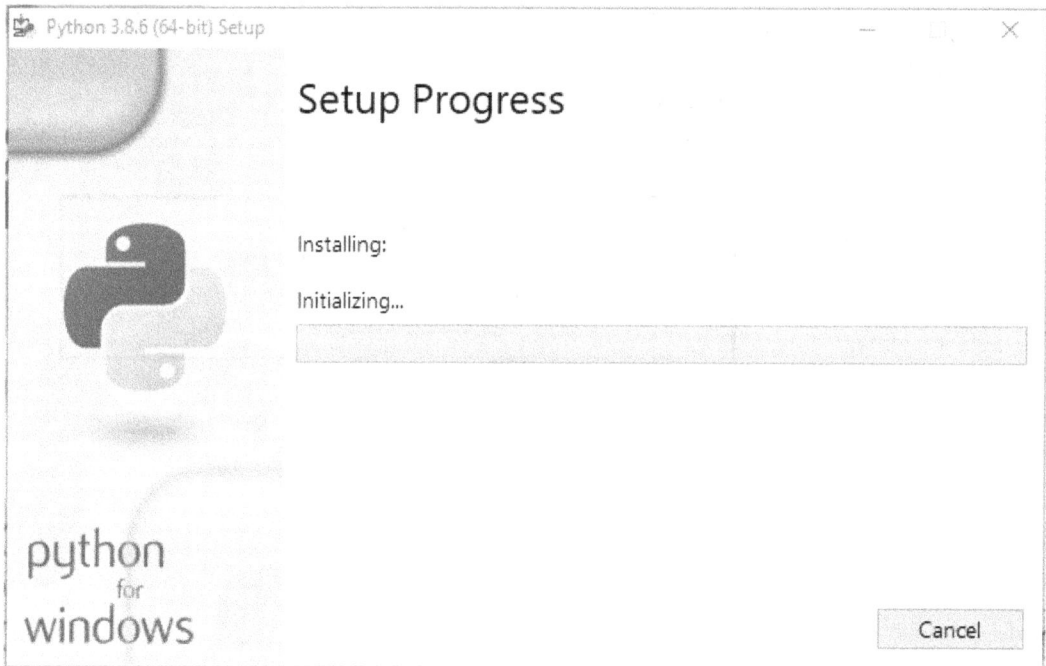

Try running python from the command prompt now. If you're using Python 3, use the python -version.

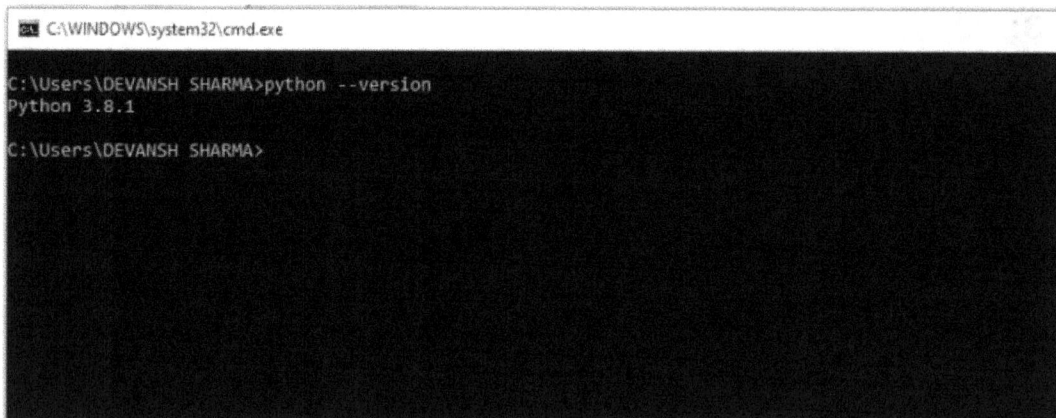

We're all set to work with Python.

Basic hints and tips to help you become a smart developer

Following are the helpful tricks for newbies:

1) Swapping numbers:

When it refers to algorithms and data structures, swapping is a crucial topic. Let's look at how to swap numbers in Python.

The Conventional Approach:

Here, we'll have to make a temporary variable to store values so that the other one can become empty and the values can be swapped.

```
x=5
y=10
temp=x
x=y
y=temp
print("The value of x after swapping is",x)
print("The value of y after swapping is",y)
```

Now, I'll show you a quick way to swap figures in Python.

```
x = 5
y = 10
x, y = y, x
print("The value of x after swapping is",x)
print("The value of y after swapping is",y)
```

2) Reversing a String

Reversing a string can't get much easier than this, so be careful. We'll utilize a basic negative indexing and string slicing approach. We see that Python may have negative indexes, so we slice it and don't provide a beginning or ending value; instead, we provide a range of -1, which means it will reverse the indexes from the last to the first.

```
word = "orehgnimmargorp"
print(word[: : -1])
```

Result:

programming hero

Simple slicing is sufficient to complete the task.

3) String Concatenation

It is among the most valuable and practical tips. Let's look at how to make a string out of a set of characters The join() function will be used. Let's have a glance at how it works.

```
characters = ['p', 'y', 't', 'h', 'o', 'n']
word = "".join(characters)
print(word)
```

Result:

Python

4) Using ZIP with lists

To merge numerous lists with the equal length and output the result, use the zip() method.

```
language = ["python", "java", "c"]
creators = ["guido van rossum", "james gosling", "denis ricthie"]
for language, creators in zip(language, creators):
    print(language, creators)
```

Result:

```
python guido van rossum
java james gosling
c denis ricthie
```

5) The _ Operator

It's possible that you've never heard of the operator before. An output of the last performed expression is represented by. Let's have a look at how it works.

```
>>> 2+ 3
5
>>> _      # the _ operator, it will return the output of the last executed statement.
>>> 5
```

6) Creating a dictionary from a list

When working on actual Machine learning and Django projects, this is one of the most effective strategies. As previously, use the zip() method, but this time use it from the dictionary function Object().

```
user = ["Peter", "John", "Sam"]
age = [23,19,34]
dictionary = dict(zip(user, age))
print(dictionary)
```

Result:

```
{"Peter" : 23, "John" : 23, "Sam" : 34}
```

7) Opening a website

Python is really about having fun. One of the greatest methods is to use a python script to access a webpage.

```
import webbrowser
webbrowser.open("https://www.programming-hero.com/")
```

This is how a website may be launched using only one line of code.

8) Multiple users input

If you're thinking, 'It's easy, simply utilize two input functions, and we're done," you're correct. But I have a better way of accomplishing it; first, let's look at the old school method.

```
x = input("Enter a number")
y = input ("Enter another number")
print(x)
print(y)
```

The more pleasant option,

```
x, y = input("Enter a two values: ").split()
print("value of x ", x)
print("value of y: ", y)
```

The split() method allows you to obtain several inputs from a user. The supplied separator is used to divide up the provided input. If no separator is specified, any white space serves as a separator.

9) The Walrus:= Operator

One of Python's most recent features is the Walrus operator. Python 3.8 was the first version to include it. It's an expression of assignment that enables you to assign values to the expression directly.

The Conventional Approach:

```
xs = [1,2,3]
n=len(xs)
if n>2:
    print(n)
```

In the following example, first, define a list and afterward assign the length of a list to a variable called n.

With the help of walrus operators,

```
xs = [1,2,3]
if (n:=len(xs)>2):
    print(n)
```

We declare and assign a value at the same time in this case. That is the Walrus operator's power.

10) Colored Text

Are you tired of your old white and black console? This ruse is meant to save you.

```python
from termcolor import colored
print(colored("Programming Hero", "yellow"))
print(colored("Programming Hero", "red"))
```

Result:

```
Programming Hero
Programming Hero
```

11) List comprehension

In Python, list comprehension provides a beautiful approach to define and generate lists. We can make lists in the same way as we can make mathematical assertions, but only on one line. The syntax for list comprehension is more straightforward. It's a clever approach to working with lists...

The Conventional Approach:

The code below provides a series of odd square values.

```python
odd_square = []
for x in range(1, 11):
    if x % 2 == 1:
        odd_square.append(x**2)
print (odd_square)
```

How to Use List Comprehension:

In the same line, we may have an expression, a loop, and a condition. In only one line, you may write 5 lines of code. That's how you understand a list.

```
odd_square = [x ** 2 for x in range(1, 11) if x % 2 == 1]
(print odd_square)
```

12) Shutting down a computer

Let's look at how to shut down a computer with only one single line of code. We will utilize the OS module for this. It's one of Python's most significant modules, with a slew of additional features.

```
import os
os.system('shutdown -s')
```

13) Multi-args Function:

It's one of Python's coolest tricks. Let's imagine you're writing the function and you don't know how many parameters the user will provide. So, how do we define the function's parameters? Multi-args functions are used to add any amount of values given by the user. See the example below.

```
def add(*num):
    result=0
    for i in num:
        result=result+i
    return result

print(add(1,2))
print(add(1,2,3,4,5))
```

Result:

```
    3
   15
```

As a result, the multi-args function constructs a list of arguments before carrying out the action.

14) Palindrome

I'm sure you've run across this issue before. This is definitely one of the institution's most popular issues. Have you ever considered doing anything using only one line of code?

```
word = "wow"
palindrome = bool(word.find(word[: : -1]) + 1)
print(palindrome)
```

Result:

```
True
```

15) Passwords are read as user input.

Provide a positive user experience even with basic menu-based apps. To read passwords from users in terminal apps, use the getpass module.

```
username : john23
password : *******
```

Result:

```
from getpass import getpass

username = input('username : ')
password = getpass('password : ' )
```

This conceals a user input for a console's password field.

16) Fibonacci series

Oh, that's a famous coding issue at another institution. I've got another easy one-line answer for you. Amaze your instructor by throwing this code at him or her.

```
fibo = lambda n : n if n <= 1 else fibo(n-1) + fibo(n-2)
result = fibo(10)
print(result)
```

17) Measuring the Time It Takes to Execute a Task

Do you want to put your software to the test? Do you want to keep track of your performance and execution time? This function will be quite beneficial. Let's try it out.

```
import time
startTime = time.time()

# your code

endTime = time.time()
totalTime = endTime - startTime
print("Execute code is= ", totalTime)
```

The milliseconds it takes for the program to run will be output, which will aid in improving performance and modifying the code appropriately.

18) Lambda Function

Because these functions don't have names, they're also known as anonymous functions. These are commonly used for Data Science, Machine Learning, Django backends, and other fields. Let's have a look at an example of how to add two integers.

Typical Function:

```
def add(a,b):
    return a + b

add(2,3)
```

Lambda Function:

```
add = lambda a,b : a+b
add(2,3)
```

19) Tuple Manipulation

What exactly is it? How are we going to do it? How can we alter tuples if we know they're immutable? Yes, we can! Because we are programmers, we can solve any difficulty. Consider the case below.

```
tuple1=(1,2,3,4,5)
list1=list(tuple1)
list1.append(6)
tuple2=tuple(list1)
print(tuple2)
```

Result:

```
(1,2,3,4,5,6)
```

Is it really that simple? It's as simple as using the list() and tuple() constructors.

20) Getting rid of duplicates in a List:

Duplicate items are possible in lists. However, there are times when duplicate entries in the list are undesirable. Let's have a look at how it can be accomplished.

```
listNumbers = [20, 22, 24, 26, 28, 28, 20, 30, 24]
print("Original= ", listNumbers)
listNumbers = list(set(listNumbers))
print("After removing duplicate= ", listNumbers)
```

Result:

```
Original = [20, 22, 24, 26, 28, 28, 20, 30, 24]
After removing duplicate = [20, 22, 24, 26, 28, 30]
```

I hope these tips will help you improve your Python skills, and it was a lot of fun!

Conclusion:

Python is a high-level programming language that is dynamically semantic, interpreted, and object-oriented. Its built-in high-level data structures make it perfect for Faster Productivity and as a scripting or glue language for integrating existing components. The readability of Python's succinct, easy-to-learn syntax is prioritized, lowering software maintenance costs. Python supports modules and packages, which encourages code reuse and software modularity. For all major systems, the Python interpreter and therefore its extensive standard library are available for free download and distribution in source or binary form.

Learning how to begin programming on a computer might seem to be a daunting task. There are several other programming alternatives available, but most of them are difficult to master, take chance to sort out, and don't always do what you need. Many individuals believe that in order to reach the level of coding that they want, they must be very intelligent or have extensive coding schooling and experience. Python, on the other hand, makes programming accessible to even the most inexperienced programmer. Python has enabled it really simple to get involved with coding, whether you're a complete novice or a seasoned pro. This language is based on English, so it's simple to read, and it's free of a lot of other symbols that render coding difficult for others to understand. Furthermore, since it is a user domain, anybody may make modifications and see other scripts to make things simpler. This handbook has spent a lot of time discussing the many functions available in Python as well as how simple it is to get started as a newbie. You will discover that this procedure is simple to learn and master with a little practice. It's simple to use, works on a number of platforms, and maybe even come pre-installed on newer Mac computers. Python is an excellent place to start whether you want to learn how to program or if you want to discover a software that can accomplish a lot of things without all of the fuss. It is among the most popular programming languages, and you'll find it simple to read and understand, especially if you have no clue where to begin.

Python is widespread among programmers because it allows them to work more efficiently. Python programs are easy to troubleshoot. A segmentation fault is never caused by a bug or faulty input. An inter preter throws an exception when it encounters an error. If the program fails to capture the error, the interpreter generates a trace of stack. Python was used to create the debugger, exhibiting Python's introspective capabilities.